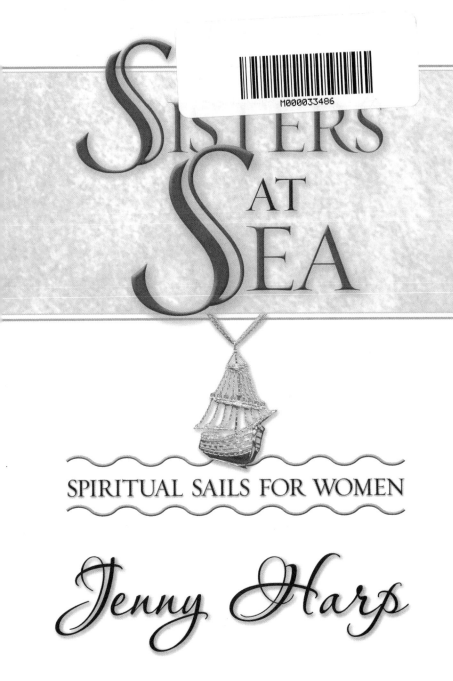

SISTERS AT SEA

SPIRITUAL SAILS FOR WOMEN

Jenny Harp

Publishing Designs, Inc.

Publishing Designs, Inc.
P.O. Box 3241
Huntsville, Alabama 35810

Page design and layout: Crosslin Creative
Images: DollarPhotoClub, VectorStock

Printed in the United States of America

Publisher's Cataloging-in-Publication

Harp, Jennifer Hubbard, 1961—

Sisters at Sea / Jenny Harp

Thirteen chapters, thought questions, activities.

1. Christian life. 2. Encouragement for righteousness. 3. Survival in life's events.

I. Harp, Jenny. II. Title

ISBN 978-0-929540-94-8

248.8

TO DAD

Captain E. L. Hubbard

You inspired this book. You dreamed about building a yacht. And you built a one-ton, thirty-foot boat with a keel.

You taught me to pursue my dreams with hard work. Your only training was a wood-work class at school.

Our weekends were spent sailing up and down the coast of the beautiful Bay of Plenty, New Zealand. The dolphins played on the bows. My memories of childhood are sunny days, salty air, and blue skies kissed by rolling waves.

Thank you, Dad. My dream is to write, and this is the product of what you taught me.

Eternal Father

Eternal Father, strong to save,
Whose arm hath bound the restless wave,
Who bidd'st the mighty ocean deep
Its own appointed limits keep;
Oh, hear us when we cry to Thee,
For those in peril on the sea!

O Christ! Whose voice the waters heard
And hushed their raging at Thy word,
Who walked'st on the foaming deep,
And calm amidst its rage didst sleep;
Oh, hear us when we cry to Thee,
For those in peril on the sea!

Most Holy Spirit!
Who didst brood
Upon the chaos dark and rude,
And bid its angry tumult cease,
And give, for wild confusion, peace;
Oh, hear us when we cry to Thee,
For those in peril on the sea!

O Trinity of love and power!
Our brethren shield in danger's hour;
From rock and tempest, fire and foe,
Protect them wheresoe'er they go;
Thus evermore shall rise to Thee
Glad hymns of praise from land and sea.

—William Whiting, 1860

CONTENTS

ENDORSEMENTS

Jenny Harp tackles Bible study from a seafaring perspective. Each "ship" chapter within *Sisters at Sea* shares common nautical themes of survival, service, and example. Readers will appreciate Jenny's research, thought-provoking scripture, practical questions, and activities that encourage diving deep into the Living Water.

But there is more. Smooth sailing, even for the Christian, is non-existent. So the chapters end with a "Shipwreck," splintering in real life. What if we are late boarding *Fellowship* or *Partnership*? What if *Membership* launches with enemy sails?

Sisters at Sea is as easy to digest as candy on the Good Ship Lollipop, and seasickness is no concern. Climb aboard.

—Peggy Coulter, editor
Publishing Designs, Inc.

Life is much like sailing on a vast sea of experiences and relationships. Calm waters are always our preference, but often winds and storms toss our ships of life into deep distress. In this book, my loving wife Jenny Harp examines various "ships" and shows us how each can be strengthened according to the blueprints from the Master Shipbuilder.

I met and fell in love with Jenny Hubbard in 1981 while working with a mission effort in Jenny's homeland, New Zealand. We married July 24, 1982. Through the years she enhanced our home with her creativity and devotion. Plus she gave me three wonderful children. Jenny has never met a stranger and comes off as a bit of a comic at times. However, her fun-loving side is beautifully balanced by her deep faith and devotion to God and His word. Her book brings a unique dimension of Bible understanding and spiritual application for your own personal ship of study.

—Scott Harp

_I_NTRODUCTION

Imagine floating on your back, arms outstretched, and rhythmically rising and falling with the motion of the ocean. Slowly close your eyes. Now open them just enough so that the light begins to dance. Relax.

When I was a little girl, that's what I imagined God to be like—the ocean—all-powerful, all-loving. He was the sea. He gently rocked me and hugged me. Was I imagining the biblical God? No, not Him. Just God. I did not grow up in a family of worshipers, so I formed my concept of God through nature. But not all was lost. I knew enough about His nature to know that He was in charge; I had to obey such an entity. Obey the rules of the ocean, and salt and rhythm would be mine. Or I could choose to flout those laws and live with the consequences—storms, crashing waves of indescribable power, and who knows what else? At least, that's how I saw it.

As I grew older, natural curiosity coupled with my innate spiritual cravings led me to examine various denominations within the "Christian" perspective. I was bewildered by all the different beliefs. I was in a fog and remained so until I began a serious study of the Bible with dedicated Christians, friends who believed only the Bible. Little by little the fog began to lift. The Savior of mankind with His simple plan of salvation began to shine through. In the book of Acts, men and women seeking salvation became examples to me. They were lost souls finding salvation in Christ. I saw the wisdom of following their lead, doing what they did to put on Christ. _The Bible is indeed a map to heaven,_ I uttered to myself somewhere along the way. I saw the importance of doing what God wanted, so I abandoned man-made ideas. And so began my fascinating quest not only to get on the road to heaven myself but to help as many as I could to come along with me. All the while I knew that the Bible was quite daunting to study, so I purposed to pretend to write a book so I would study more deeply.

From as far back as I remember, I have loved the sea. My dad would take us aboard ships, and it was exciting to embrace a new culture as I crossed the "gangplank." Those experiences helped me with the theme of this book. Thanks, Dad!

So come go on a journey with me, a seafaring journey. Our ship—oops, ships!—are the vessels of the Bible: partnership, swordsmanship, and stewardship to name a few.

May God bless us on our journey as we stroll along the deck and watch the wheeling gulls sweeping overhead and gliding just above the waves. We will stand at the ship's bow watching sleek shiny dolphins arching and skimming over the white water. This study is designed to help you come to know better the God of all glory and His Son our Savior. Then you will know that "every good gift and every perfect gift is from above, coming down from the Father of lights, with whom there is no variation or shadow due to change" (James 1:17).

Jenny Harp

June 15, 2015

CHAPTER ONE

PARTNERSHIP
PRAYER AND STUDY

I peered so intently through the viewfinder to get the best shot that I forgot I was standing on the next to the top step of a stairway. So when I stepped back to widen my field of vision, my feet flew out from under me and my seat dropped with a thud onto that top step. Unable to regain my balance, I bounced to the next step, then the next, then the—got the picture? My body seemed to slide along the surface of a slanted sea, accelerating at the crest of each rock-hard wave. Before I could say "New Zealand," I hit the bottom and came to an abrupt halt on a cobblestone path.

I'll never be able to sit down again, I moaned as I turned on my side to find relief from the pain. *I need somebody—just anybody—to help me to my feet.* Then the reality of it all hit me and I started to laugh. Who would I ask for help? I was in my jammies and my greatest injury was to my pride.

GOD'S PARTNER

Two are better than one, because they have a good reward for their toil. For if they fall, one will lift up his fellow. But woe to him who is alone when he falls and has not another to lift him up! (Ecclesiastes 4:9–10).

So we need a partner, and the greatest one of all is God.

> You are the Lord, you alone. You have made heaven, the heaven of heavens, with all their host, the earth and all that is on it, the seas and all that is in them; and you preserve all of them; and the host of heaven worships you (Nehemiah 9:6).

How do we form a partnership with God? Let's examine this deep question in light of prayer and study. Prayer is our upward plea, praise, petition, and thanks to God. But if you have ever tried to talk on a cell phone with a friend when reception is poor, you know how frustrating one-way communication can be. "Hello, can you hear me?" "Barely. Y—are brea—k—g up. Can you—me?" That is what prayer is like without Bible study—an attempt to question, petition, and thank someone with whom we cannot communicate. Conversely, if we study without prayer we learn about God, but we cannot have the personal relationship with Him that we need.

WHY MUST PRAYER AND STUDY BE PARTNERS?

Because of the Human Condition

Becky Blackmon, author of *The Begging Place*, reminded me of a great scripture from Solomon's pen:

> He has made everything beautiful in its time. Also, he has put eternity into man's heart, yet so that he cannot find out what God has done from the beginning to the end (Ecclesiastes 3:11).

We—God's little insignificant creatures—have eternity in our hearts! We have a God-breathed essence, a soul within us that yearns to understand. Yet we are bound to the physical confines of a mortal body whose only constant is its rapid acceleration toward death.

What is another word for *beautiful* in Ecclesiastes 3:11?

_____

How does Ecclesiastes 3:11 apply to the aging process?

_____

But the death we fear, the death that Hollywood portrays as the Grim Specter, is really a blessing. What if Adam and Eve, after eating the forbidden fruit, had eaten of the tree of life? It seems to me they would have been forever chained to the physical realm, never to die—doomed, never to unite spiritually with God. They would be living a hopeless, havenless existence.

> Then the Lord God said, "Behold, the man has become like one of us in knowing good and evil. Now, lest he reach out his hand and take also of the tree of life and eat, and live forever—" therefore the Lord God sent him out from the garden of Eden to work the ground from which he was taken. He drove out the man, and at the east of the garden of Eden he placed the cherubim and a flaming sword that turned every way to guard the way to the tree of life (Genesis 3:22–24).

Add to this Paul's admonition: "For now we see in a mirror dimly, but then face to face. Now I know in part; then I shall know fully, even as I have been fully known" (1 Corinthians 13:12).

Our God, Father, and Creator, wants to mold us for heaven. He has given us the assurance of His listening ear so we can go to Him in prayer. Then we can go to the Bible so we can know better how to pray. The more we utilize both prayer and Bible study, the better fitted we will be for heaven.

What words in Genesis 3:22 indicate that God's plan was for man to die physically?

_____

Because We Have Needs

Prayer and Bible study belong with our daily steps. Yes, our desires confront us by the minute. However, our real needs—food, clothing, and shelter—don't usually eat away at our thoughts. Only when we have a "true need" crisis do we feel the gut-wrenching dependence to trust that God will provide. Faith-building Bible study is the bedrock of confident prayer.

> Ask, and it will be given to you; seek, and you will find; knock, and it will be opened to you. For everyone who asks receives, and the one who seeks finds, and to the one who knocks it will be opened. Or which one of you, if his son asks him for bread, will give him a stone? Or if he asks for a fish, will give him a serpent? If you then, who are evil, know how to give good gifts to your children, how much more will your Father who is in heaven give good things to those who ask him! (Matthew 7:7–11).

He then tells us how to ask. We are to ask in faith. This exemplifies our partnership with prayer and study because faith comes from hearing the word of God (Romans 10:17). When we pray in faith, we pray according to God's will, and that truly is best for us.

> If any of you lacks wisdom, let him ask God, who gives generously to all without reproach, and it will be given him. But let him ask in faith, with no doubting, for the one who doubts is like a wave of the sea that is driven and tossed by the wind (James 1:5–6).

The writer is telling us to ask the One most able to supply our needs. He also tells us what to request—wisdom.

Take an inventory of your personal prayer life, as well as the past month of prayers in worship. What is the ratio of prayers for physical needs compared to those of spiritual needs? Discuss which is more important.

_____

_____

"I have been young, and now am _____, yet I have not seen the _____ forsaken or his children begging for bread" (Psalm 37:25).

Solomon asked for an answer to a spiritual need, wisdom. He had a huge burden. His father was dead, and he was left to govern Israel. It was a daunting task for which Solomon felt completely inadequate. Let us examine his prayer.

At Gibeon the Lord appeared to Solomon in a dream by night, and God said, "Ask what I shall give you." And Solomon said, "You have shown great and steadfast love to your servant David my father, because he walked before you in faithfulness, in righteousness, and in uprightness of heart toward you. And you have kept for him this great and steadfast love and have given him a son to sit on his throne this day. And now, O Lord my God, you have made your servant king in place of David my father, although I am but a little child. I do not know how to go out or come in. And your servant is in the midst of your people whom you have chosen, a great people, too many to be numbered or counted for multitude. Give your servant therefore an understanding mind to govern your people, that I may discern between good and evil, for who is able to govern this your great people?" It pleased the Lord that Solomon had asked this. And God said to him, "Because you have asked this, and

PRAYER AND BIBLE STUDY BELONG WITH OUR DAILY STEPS.

have not asked for yourself long life or riches or the life of your enemies, but have asked for yourself understanding to discern what is right, behold, I now do according to your word. Behold, I give you a wise and discerning mind, so that none like you has been before you and none like you shall arise after you. I give you also what you have not asked, both riches and honor, so that no other king shall compare with you, all your days" (1 Kings 3:5–13).

Because We Need Humbly to Seek God's Will

Solomon honored God. He recounted God's steadfastness and loving attitude toward his father David. Then he humbled himself completely before God. Jesus spoke of that spirit as He began the Sermon on the Mount: "Blessed are the poor in spirit, for theirs is the kingdom of heaven" (Matthew 5:3).

God's blessings will come on you only when you are humble in spirit and mind as Solomon was and seek God's will as Solomon did. Solomon first acknowledged God. Then he laid out his needs before God: an understanding mind to govern God's people, and wisdom to discern between good and evil. His purpose was unselfish and responsible.

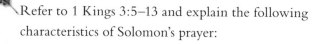

Refer to 1 Kings 3:5–13 and explain the following characteristics of Solomon's prayer:

1. He honored God.

_____

2. He recounted God's steadfastness and loving attitude toward his father David.

_____

3. He humbled himself completely before God.

_____

How did God respond? He blessed Solomon beyond all expectations. He promised to reward him with riches, honor, and a long life if he continued to do right.

God is that loving parent who gives generously to His children, but He is never the permissive parent who gives in and accepts their deeds no matter what they do. God is not mocked. He expects His children to keep His commandments for their own good.

Notice also that God's blessings never forced Solomon to conduct himself properly. God is not the controlling parent. He does not force love or obedience. He gives us the tools for success and lets us choose.

Read 1 Corinthians 10:13 and answer the following questions:

1. How is temptation "common to man"?

_____

2. What is God's solution to temptation?

_____

3. Explain this phrase: "that you may be able to endure it." How does that phrase clarify that God expects us to struggle?

_____

Because We Too Are Little Ones

Solomon prayed to God and studied His word. David taught him the way of righteousness when he was a young child (Proverbs 4:3–27). At his father's feet, Solomon learned to prize wisdom above all else. His learning God's word, partnered with his dedication to prayer, formed the foundation for wisdom, so when God said, "Ask what I shall give you." Solomon's heartfelt request was for an understanding heart to judge His people and to discern good and evil. He longed to be wise.

Here is a song based on Proverbs 3:5–6:

> Trust in the Lord with all your heart;
> Lean not on your own understanding.
> In all your ways acknowledge him,
> And he will make your paths straight.

Rebecca Harp Hooper, Kyle Hooper, Emma Skype Hooper

Mothers, do not underestimate your power for good with your little ones. Teach them to pray. Sing Bible verses to them, such as the one above. Make up your own. I put Genesis 1 to song, and my grown kids can still sing it. Strive to be wise mothers who encourage your children to long for wisdom.

1. How do we know that someone is wise?

_____

2. Proverbs 9:8–9: "Reprove a _____ man, and he will love you. Give instruction to a _____ man, and he will be still wiser."

3. Proverbs 11:2: "With the humble is _____."

4. Proverbs 12:15: "A _____ man listens to advice."

5. Proverbs 14:16: "One who is _____ is cautious and turns away from evil."

So ladies, let's be humble, listen well to advice, and take in instruction. Let's be cautious and turn away from evil. Let's be wise!

Because Prayer and Study Help Us To Be Constant and Habitual

We know that we must pray in line with God's word, so we must study God's word. He made us. He made us spirit beings as well as physical ones. He has given us the key that fits the eternity-shaped keyhole in our hearts. Turn that key by turning the pages of the Bible.

Pray without ceasing (1 Thessalonians 5:17).

Do your best to present yourself to God as one approved, a worker who has no need to be ashamed, rightly handling the word of truth (2 Timothy 2:15).

> **Approved**—accepted, particularly of coins. Dishonest merchants shaved the coins to collect the precious metal. Money changers usually passed those coins off at full value. But some of the changers carefully weighed all coins and rejected the devalued ones. The Greeks called such a merchant *dokimos* (tested, approved).

The challenge facing busy Christian women is having enough study time to do our work and raise kids. How can we take time for such a luxury? I had three children in three years: three kids in diapers at the same time, in case you missed that—mothers didn't! My study was incidental, so I had to improvise. I memorized scripture and rehearsed those verses throughout the day, so folding clothes and washing dishes were Bible study and meditation opportunities.

Circle the commands in 2 Timothy 2:15. Why do we sometimes think we are exempt from these commands? What excuses do we make for our failure to obey them?

_____

_____

~~~~~ MAKE STUDY A GIFT ~~~~~

When Brooke, our youngest, was six months old and the twins were three, I attended International Bible College, now Heritage Christian University, with my husband. The children stayed in the nursery while Scott and I attended class. Jim Massey taught us how to use the Bible as its own commentary. Because of his godly influence, to this day I write in the margins of my study Bible what each chapter is about, and I cross-reference verses. I also have made up color codes that show the themes of the scriptures in various passages. Each verse on forgiveness, for example, is blue and yellow. This makes subjects easy to find.

Years later I attended a Bible class taught by Becky Blackmon. Becky's constant companion was her mother's Bible, and not one class went by without her referencing something her mother had written in the margin of her Bible. She would say, "I have my mother's thoughts right here."

I purposed then and there to let my Bible be a gift of thought for my own children. I use a wide margin Bible and skinny, skinny pens. It will be a blessing to them to learn what their daddy, my preacher, said on so many occasions. For me, writing notes in separate books is not as good as writing in my Bible. Books get lost on shelves and gather dust, whereas the Christian woman's Bible is seen and used daily, so place the notes where they will always be before you.

Every mother should make Bible study and prayer her abiding partners.

I know that if I am teaching a class I will study harder. So even if I am not teaching, I imagine I am. That makes study purposeful. Every mother should make Bible study and prayer her abiding partners. Embrace these partners and discover smoother sailing on your glorious journey on the sea of life.

SHIPWRECK

All the Canaanites knew the power of the God of Israel, and they feared Him. God and Israel were partners. When the neighboring Gibeonites heard what Joshua had done to Jericho and Ai, they were afraid and cunningly set out to trick Joshua. They gathered dry and crumbly provisions and took worn-out sacks for their donkeys, worn-out and patched wineskins, worn-out clothes, and old sandals. Then they went to nearby Gilgal to meet with Joshua and trick him into believing they were from a tribe out of the area.

"We have come from a distant country," they lied, "so now make a covenant with us."

"Perhaps you live among us," Joshua replied. "Then how can I make a covenant with you?"

"We are your servants," they told Joshua. "From a very distant country your servants have come, because of the name of the Lord your God. For we have heard a report of him, and all that he did in Egypt."

DON'T TAKE ON A PARTNER WITHOUT ASKING YOUR FATHER.

Joshua was skeptical, so his men thoroughly investigated the matter. They examined the old provisions. The strangers seemed to be telling the truth. So Joshua made a covenant with them and swore to them assuring them of peaceful habitation. Three days later, Joshua learned the truth, but because of the oath, Israel could not harm the Gibeonites.

Shipwreck! Israel was "taking in water," but the damage could not be repaired. When the Gibeonites' lies were exposed, Joshua observed, "We have sworn to them by the Lord, the God of Israel."

The Gibeonites became cutters of wood and drawers of water, and lived among the Israelites. They became a thorn in Israel's side. Years later Saul attacked the Gibeonites. Then during David's reign, a three-year famine sent David to his knees.

The Lord rebuked David: "There is bloodguilt on Saul and on his house because he put the Gibeonites to death."

To atone for Israel's breaking of their covenant, the Gibeonites requested seven descendants of Saul. All of them were hanged. (See 2 Samuel 21:3–9.)

When partnership is shipwrecked, the consequences are not ending; they are just beginning. The flotsam and jetsam of carnage may float on for generations, as with Israel and David.

The take-home thought? Don't take on a partner without asking your Father.

SHIP'S LOG

1. List some of your most memorable prayers.

2. Select a verse and make it a theme prayer for a year. Proverbs 3:5–6 took me to some amazing places as I prayed, "Lord God, please direct my steps."

3. Take baby steps. Learn one verse, study one chapter, and pray for wisdom. You will be blessed by doing so (James 1:5).

4. Keep a prayer journal with specific prayers. Repeatedly praying for "the sick and afflicted the world over" can easily become a ritual that does not glorify God. But praying for "Mary Jones, my

neighbor down the street" and receiving an answer does glorify our Father and shows us how He is working in our lives.

5. Share some prayers with class members.

~~~~~~~~~~ *Conduit* ~~~~~~~~~~

I
Want to try
To be a conduit

Through me run the word of God
Stream it through my heart Lord
Let someone "see"

For Christ was born
And lived and died
God and man
He satisfied

If Christ be lifted up
He will draw all to Him

Help me
Lift Him up
In what I
Try

CHAPTER TWO

STEWARDSHIP
BOUGHT WITH A PRICE

Our voyage continues beneath a stretched-out and beautiful blue canopy. The sun is fierce, burnishing the sea like a shining shield.

I am from New Zealand. The Maori called it Aotearoa, meaning "the land of the long white cloud." The original settlers, thought to be Polynesians, arrived more than seven hundred years ago in outrigger canoes. What a journey! They traversed the huge Pacific Ocean, guided by stars at night. The Maori people always believed the earth was round. Gaze long enough at the horizon and you will see the curvature of the earth.

YOU'RE THE MANAGER, NOT THE BOSS

We are on board a new vessel *Stewardship*. She docks alongside her sister *Ownership*. Stewardship is a difficult concept for our modern minds to grasp because we love our independence and even celebrate it. The English word *stewardship* is translated from the Greek word *oikonomeo*, "to manage a house or estate, to steward." A steward is a manager, an overseer, or an employee.

When I was growing up, my friend's dad was a farm manager. He worked the farm for the owner. He lived on the land and used its produce to provide for his family, but none of these things were his. He was the steward.

> **Steward**—a manager to whom the head of the house or proprietor has entrusted the management of his affairs, the care of receipts and expenditures, and the duty of dealing out the proper portion to every servant and even to the children not yet of age; the manager of a farm or landed estate, an overseer.

In J. R. R. Tolkien's trilogy, *The Lord of the Rings*, Denethor was the Steward of Gondor. He was from a long line of stewards, but the people had always looked for a king. Denethor had immense power, so when he heard that Aragorn was the rightful king of Gondor, he said, "Gondor does not need a king!" Denethor did not want to relinquish his power.

Does that sound familiar? Jesus was the rightful king of the Jews, the Messiah, the Christ, their Savior, but the stiff-necked, hard-hearted Jews did not want to give up their power. So it is very important that we get the right concept of stewardship, because God's plan is so beautiful for us.

> For I know the plans I have for you, declares the Lord, plans for welfare and not for evil, to give you a future and a hope (Jeremiah 29:11).

OWNERSHIP

We cannot understand stewardship until we understand ownership.

> For none of us lives to himself, and none of us dies to himself. For if we live, we live to the Lord, and if we die, we die to the Lord. So then, whether we live or whether we die, we are the Lord's (Romans 14:7–8).

Do you hear it? Do you hear Paul's triumphant shout, ringing loudly for all time? We are the Lord's! We belong to Him! Stewardship means that I have a Master and Lord. It colors everything in my life, and so it is who I am. Also, He has given me a task. And He will return.

> For it is written, "As I live, says the Lord, every knee shall bow to me, and every tongue shall confess to God." So then each of us will give an account of himself to God (Romans 14:11–12).

From scripture give an example of both a good steward and a bad steward.

_____

_____

Ezekiel 18:4 says, "Behold all souls are _____." Who is speaking? How does this verse defy the protest, "I can do what I want; it's my life!"

_____

~~~~ HE OWNS MY BODY ~~~~

Because we are a temple of the Holy Spirit, we must keep our bodies pure.

> Or do you not know that your body is a temple of the Holy Spirit within you, whom you have from God? You are not your own, for you were bought with a price. So glorify God in your body (1 Corinthians 6:19–20).

Immorality is the sin about which the Holy Spirit through Paul sternly warns us:

Flee from sexual immorality. Every other sin a person commits is outside the body, but the sexually immoral person sins against his own body (1 Corinthians 6:18).

Thank God for that warning. We could never have figured it out on our own!

We must urge our young people to stay pure so their marriages will be blessed. Physical attraction is not love. Sex is not love. A person can, and often is, attracted to a person who is not compatible—and never will be. We must teach our children to be good stewards of their bodies.

∼∼∼ BUFFET THE BODY ∼∼∼

Our bodies are the temple of the Holy Spirit, and yet some of us stuff them too often with junk food and drink at an all-you-can-eat buffet. God instructed His people in days of old in ways that promoted good health. Even into his old days, Moses was very healthy. He began his exodus from Egypt at eighty years of age. Then he worked another forty years.

CHRISTIANS SHOULD BE THE HEALTHIEST PEOPLE ON THE PLANET.

We too can be healthy. Eat plenty of fruits and vegetables, especially leafy green ones. Use good fats. (I cook with grape seed oil and butter. I use olive oil for dressings.) Avoid processed food and sugar. Eat fiber! Chia seeds are good on just about everything. These humble little seeds have 8,400 ORAC units per tablespoon. They detoxify you and give you tons of energy. Also, they absorb ten to thirty times their weight in water, creating a full feeling and inhibiting the craving for sweets.

Christians should be the healthiest people on the planet. I have always enjoyed pursuing foods, attitudes, and exercises that promote good health. Unfortunately, the sick lists in our bulletins loudly proclaim that we are not as healthy as we should be. So determine to embrace stewardship in your own body and strive, like Paul, to buffet your body and keep it in subjection. And that does not mean we should stuff ourselves at an all-you-can-eat restaurant!

"But I _____ my body and keep it under _____, lest after preaching to others I myself should be disqualified" (1 Corinthians 9:27).

Consider how much time, expense, and stress will be avoided in the church when each Christian takes personal responsibility for her own health. List diseases that can be avoided by the discipline mentioned in 1 Corinthians 9:27.

_____

_____

~~~~ MANAGE YOUR MONEY ~~~~

Stewardship is best understood in our giving, especially since God has given us the ability to earn money. He created everything and provided all things we have, so we should give to Him with that in mind.

Have you read what the prophet Malachi wrote about giving? Yes, Malachi is a book in the Old Testament, but it teaches a principle that never changes.

Will man rob God? Yet you are robbing me. But you say, "How have we robbed you?" In your tithes and contributions. You are cursed with a curse, for you are robbing me, the whole nation of you. Bring the full tithe into the storehouse, that there may be food in my house. And thereby put me to the test, says the Lord of hosts, if I will not open the windows of heaven for you and pour down for you a blessing until there is no more need. I will rebuke the devourer for you, so that it will not destroy the fruits of your soil, and your vine in the field shall not fail to bear, says the Lord of hosts (Malachi 3:8–12).

In Malachi 3:10, God says, "Put Me to the test." Comment on this statement. See if you can find another place in the Bible where God asks people to test Him.

Discuss the "full tithe" mentioned in Malachi 3:10? See Malachi 1:6–14.

When we give fully, what happens? (Malachi 3:10).

Think of how much we as parents want to delight in our children whom we love. God is our parent. He delights in our giving to Him, as we delight when our little one brings us a beautiful wild flower or pours us an imaginary cup of tea, offering her best. In a similar manner, God loves our gifts when He can see our loving hearts and our faces smiling toward Him. The only acceptable gift is our whole heart, broken, contrite, and fully aware of His infinite sacrifice for us. We are nothing without Him! Remember, God looks on the heart and not as man looks. Read it for yourself in 1 Samuel 16:7.

Jesus Himself made a profound statement about giving.

Give, and it will be given to you. Good measure, pressed down, shaken together, running over, will be put into your lap. For with the measure you use it will be measured back to you (Luke 6:38).

~~~~~ WHAT TO GIVE? ~~~~~

When Scott and I were planning our marriage, we agreed that when we had children, I would stay home with them. We thank God that He has made that possible. I have loved being with them. Yet every Sunday I felt sad when the collection plate was passed. I knew that Scott's income was mine, and what I put into the collection plate was my contribution. But I still felt as if I needed to give something that came from my labor. Even the widow gave her mites. What I put into the plate was not from my earnings. So each time the plate was passed, I prayed to dedicate myself and my children to the Lord. Now when I see my adult children, I know God heard my heartfelt plea. This is the good measure, pressed down, shaken together, and running over kind of gift.

When our son Richard was ten, he received twenty-five dollars for his birthday. He decided to put it all into the collection plate, even though to him twenty-five dollars was a small fortune. I have since told him that God saw his pure heart. The blessings he has received in his adult life are the "Luke 6:38" kind, as a direct result of his giving spirit.

WE ARE OWNED BY GOD.

We are stewards because we are owned by God. We must be good stewards, for one day the Owner will return, and we must be wholeheartedly one hundred percent God's women to receive the ultimate blessing of heaven.

SHIPWRECK

The Ship Can Go Aground

There's a resounding alarm.
They cry, "All hands on
    deck!"
Steward-ship is going down;
Our ship is about to wreck.
We're stewards of our bodies;
We should be in such good
    health.
We think stewardship is
Just about using our wealth.
What about the junk we stuff
Into our bodies each day?

Learn what causes diseases;
Always keep that food away!
Sugar is linked to cancer;
Aspartame is poisonous.
We have to be wise stewards,
Or the end will be heinous.
The ships we are have been
    bought;
We're stewards of mind and
    limb.
We're bought by His sacrifice;
Our bodies belong to Him.

**SHIP'S
LOG**

1. Discuss some creative ways we can give.

2. How do we teach our children to be good stewards?

3. How are you being a good steward of your body?

4. We have the fulfillment of Christ's sacrifice in our lives. How
   does your giving compare with Israel's giving in Malachi's day?

CHAPTER THREE

KINSHIP
JESUS AND JAMES

Imagine two boys sitting on the shore of the Sea of Galilee skimming stones. They watch as the waves dash to and fro on the rocks, driven by the wind. As the sun sinks in the west, the boys cast long shadows on the gritty sand. The taller boy turns to the other, points to their shadows, and observes, "God does not have one of those. He is the Father of lights."

James, whose shadow is the shorter and smaller, then asks, "Can you tell me more about God?"

"Well," says the older boy, Jesus, "He is the giver of every good and perfect gift. He has no variation or shifting shadow because He is light."

"No shadow?" asks James. "I cannot imagine that!"

WAS THE BOY LOST?

The scriptures do not give such a rendering, but doesn't your mind wonder as it ponders what it would have been like to be a brother to Jesus? We do not know when James realized that Jesus was the Messiah. We do not know much about our Savior's early life, but let us look at what scripture does tell us.

And the child grew and became strong, filled with wisdom. And the favor of God was upon him. Now his parents went to Jerusalem every year at the Feast of the Passover. And when he was twelve years old, they went up according to custom. And when the feast was ended, as they were returning, the boy Jesus stayed behind in Jerusalem. His parents did not know it, but supposing him to be in the group they went a day's journey, but then they began to search for him among their relatives and acquaintances, and when they did not find him, they returned to Jerusalem, searching for him. After three days they found him in the temple, sitting among the teachers, listening to them and asking them questions. And all who heard him were amazed at his understanding and his answers. And when his parents saw him, they were astonished. And his mother said to him, "Son, why have you treated us so? Behold, your father and I have been searching for you in great distress." And he said to them, "Why were you looking for me? Did you not know that I must be in my Father's house?" And they did not understand the saying that he spoke to them. And he went down with them and came to Nazareth and was submissive to them. And his mother treasured up all these things in her heart. And Jesus increased in wisdom and in stature and in favor with God and man (Luke 2:40–52).

> **Passover**—On the eve of their departure from Egyptian slavery, God instructed the Israelites to prepare a lamb and put its blood on the lentils and doorposts of their houses. They were to "observe this rite as a statute for you and for your sons forever." They could later explain to their children that on the night God struck the Egyptians, He "passed over" His people.

The sentiments of verse 40 are also recorded in verse 19: "But Mary kept all these things and pondered them in her heart" (Luke 2:19 NKJV).

Review Luke 2:40–52 and list some of the emotions Mary likely experienced as she and Joseph searched for Jesus and as He grew up in their house.

_____

_____

What a precious mother she was. Mary surely did not brag that she and Joseph were raising the Savior of mankind. She did not scream across the playground: "Leave him alone; He is the Son of God!" No, Mary kept things treasured up inside her, so Jesus had the most normal upbringing He could have. Therefore, it is safe to assume that Jesus' siblings were not taught at their mother's knee that their elder brother was the Messiah.

HIS OWN HOUSEHOLD

Matthew tells us that His countrymen "took offense at him." But Jesus said to them, "A prophet is not without honor except in his hometown and in his own household" (Matthew 13:57). It would appear that initially Jesus' siblings did not believe He was the Messiah, but because of James' authorship of the book of James and the fact that Matthew mentions James in connection with Jesus, we know that later he believed and became a powerful force for God. (See Matthew 13:54–58.)

James could not bring himself to believe his brother was the Messiah. Have you ever thought that perhaps the reason James talks about the tongue being a fire is because of things he had said to Jesus that never could be taken back? (See James 3.) Words scar, and we can only guess at the angry accusations James had hurled at Jesus. But eventually James was converted.

I know that any reference to an unrecorded event in the early life of Jesus is mere conjecture, but it is fascinating to contemplate His early years. How He must have loved to smell the wood shavings as He watched His dad Joseph make household articles!

IN HIS LINEAGE, THERE IS NO PARTIALITY.

My dad built boats. He hand-planed and hand-routed the planks of wood, fitting them like ribs to a boat's backbone. I stood transfixed as the boat grew. And, of course, I helped.

Maybe Joseph's boys helped him build vessels. Maybe James watched Joseph craft the rudder and marveled at how small it was compared to the large size of the ship. (See James 3:4.)

Can you feel a kinship with James? His affinity with nature strikes a chord with me, especially since I grew up by the sea. I see the waves tossing to and fro, and the sun rising with a scorching heat.

James' true kinship was with Jesus, but he never mentions it. Rather, he said that he was a servant of God, and of the Lord Jesus Christ. What humility!

KIN TO JESUS

The truly wonderful thing about the love and generosity of God is that even though James and Jude had kinship to Jesus on earth, they also had the promise of eternal kinship. And that is wonderful for us, for we will share that eternal kinship with them.

What a family we have in Christ! God is our loving Father who brings us good gifts. It might sound strange but, as a child, I rather enjoyed being sick because my father always bought me a gift to cheer me up. When I had the mumps he gave me *Black Beauty*. But that pales in comparison to what God gives: every good gift and every perfect gift (James 1:17).

Our heavenly Father is our example. Do you see the little boy mimicking his dad as he sits at his computer? Dad crosses his legs and waggles his foot a little. His son copies every move. This is adorable in our two- and three-year-olds. God finds it adorable in us, too, when we mimic Him by putting James 1:27 into action.

James 1:27: Religion that is pure and undefiled before God, the Father, is this:

_____

_____

God our Father is merciful and non-partial. So should we be. "For judgment is without mercy to one who has shown no mercy. Mercy triumphs over judgment" (James 2:13). And the proof of God's mercy and non-partiality is a few verses down. "And in the same way was not also Rahab the prostitute justified by works when she received the messengers and sent them out by another way?" (James 2:25). Rahab, the forgiven prostitute, became a faithful ancestor of Jesus. In His lineage there is no partiality. God loves us all. No matter how stained and corrupt our lives have been, when we turn to Him, He forgives us completely. When we are in Christ, God who has no shadow, God who is pure light, and God who is pure in love can at last have a relationship with sinful men and women.

In another chapter we will explore this glorious subject in greater depth, and explain further how we can become kin to Christ in a better way than James, before he became a believer. We can be a part of the true, wondrous family of God our Father and Jesus Christ our brother and Lord.

SHIPWRECK

The ties we make with parents, sisters, brothers, grandparents, and other extended family relatives make us who we are. When family ties snap for whatever reason, the hurt can be insurmountable.

Forgiveness and love are the balm for kinship. Don't the activities and teachings of James, the half-brother of our Lord, provide evidence for this belief? Mark 3 tells of Jesus healing many people. Unclean spirits were falling down before Him and crying out, "You are the Son of God" (Mark 3:11). Jesus urged them not to make Him known. Then He went up into the mountain and called the

Dad, Edward L. Hubbard, toddler,
with his sister, Marion

disciples and appointed the twelve. But word of His miracles got around. "And when his family heard it, they went out to seize him, for they were saying, 'He is out of his mind'" (Mark 3:21).

The book of James is forgiveness in action. It is one of my favorite books, because it does much more than demonstrate a physical brotherly connection. It shows a spiritual connection of James with the Savior.

SHIP'S LOG

1. How would the world see us if we were truly following James' advice? Discuss the taming of the tongue (James 3:2) and the vapor of life (James 4:14) in light of James 1:27.

2. Explore the relationship Mary had with her boys. Think about the marvelous observations James makes about the natural world. Can you imagine Mary taking walks with them along the shore of Galilee or teaching her boys responsibility as they looked after the family donkey? I have always felt that children develop an affinity with their Creator when they observe His created nature. Discuss.

My Battle Gear

My husband is my hero
Because he preaches truth

Each week he clothes us
With armor to make us strong
We are in a battle folks
To resist the devil's wrong

Make him flee with shining sword
I have my gospel armor on
Girded with the truth
Gospel shoes of peace
And the shield of faith
I have a breastplate of noble
Righteousness

I'm in the battle not for life
But for my very soul

But with the sword of the Word
I'll stab the devil away
I'll make him flee
I am armed and I am free
I am in Christ
And His word shelters me.

CHAPTER FOUR

SWORDSMANSHIP
THE CHRISTIAN'S BATTLE

It has always fascinated me that *sword* is "word" with an "s" in front of it. According to Ephesians 6, the sword is the word of God. "And take the helmet of salvation, and the sword of the Spirit, which is the word of God" (Ephesians 6:17).

Ephesians 6 examines the armor of God and specifically swordsmanship.

> Put on the whole armor of God, that you may be able to stand against the schemes of the devil. For we do not wrestle against flesh and blood, but against the rulers, against the authorities, against the cosmic powers over this present darkness, against the spiritual forces of evil in the heavenly places. Therefore take up the whole armor of God, that you may be able to withstand in the evil day, and having done all, to stand firm (Ephesians 6:11–13).

We are in a battle against evil and we need to be prepared. God expects us to know the characteristics of our enemy.

Circle the words in the verses below that describe the devil. Discuss these verses.

> "Now the **serpent** was more crafty than any other beast of the field that the Lord God had made" (Genesis 3:1).
>
> "But I am afraid that as the serpent deceived Eve by his cunning, your thoughts will be led astray from a sincere and pure devotion to Christ" (2 Corinthians 11:3).
>
> "Put on the whole armor of God, that you may be able to stand against the schemes of the devil" (Ephesians 6:11).

Comment on "the spiritual forces of evil" (Ephesians 6:12).

_____

_____

LACK OF KNOWLEDGE CAUSES AMNESIA

It chills me to know that God will forget my darling child if I forget Him.

> My people are destroyed for lack of knowledge; because you have rejected knowledge, I reject you from being a priest to me. And since you have forgotten the law of your God, I also will forget your children (Hosea 4:6).

I don't want God to forget my children because of my lack of knowledge. What will keep me from forgetting the law of God and help me to protect my children from being abandoned by God? I must become a word-of-God-sword-wielder if I would please God. The word of God is a sword to arm us with knowledge of God to fight Satan. How are we using this sword? For the most part, we are using it lightly. I say "using it lightly" because we usually take it from the shelf only when we are on our way to worship or to Bible study. If you don't believe that, look in the Bible lost-and-found drawer at the church building. The soldier, as described in Ephesians 6, needs his sword beside him at all times. How often do we wield ours? Are we like Jesus who used scripture to defeat Satan in Matthew 4, or do we keep silent because we cannot answer our neighbor's religious arguments? Not only did Jesus defeat Satan with scripture, but He did so from memory.

Look up the hymn "Almost Persuaded" and review the lyrics. How "persuaded" is the average Christian? How important is Bible study to women who are persuaded to obey God?

_____

_____

Challenge yourself and your friends in Bible knowledge. Initiate conversation with the question, "Which Bible passage has your attention this week?" How will this impact those around you?

_____

_____

We must also commit scripture to memory, for our own battle is very real, especially for our kids in this electronic entertainment age. Sometimes we assume that our children know more than they do. But I wonder how many children have heard a sermon on instrumental music. How many are able to defend the truth on using only a cappella singing in worship? What do they believe about divorce and remarriage or women's role in public worship? Ask them.

Although I homeschooled my children, they also attended some tutored classes. I used the time when they were under a good teacher's care to teach reading with art in nine schools in Clayton county, Georgia, in the Atlanta area. I visited once a month to read and do an art activity. Of course, religion was taboo, but I told those kids that I prayed for them each week.

I drew timelines with big crosses as I read Aesop's fables. I went a step further and read the story of Jesus' birth. Sadly, some children had not heard it. I asked my director if my actions had been acceptable. She told me they had not been. But we live in America, a country built on religious freedom. Are we not seeing a people being destroyed for lack of knowledge? Open your eyes.

A cappella—literally "in the manner of the church." Music was strictly vocal in the early church. Pope Vitalian introduced organs into worship six hundred years after the church was established. The Roman church divided in AD 1054 into the Eastern church (Constantinople, now Istanbul) and Western church (Rome) over many issues, music being one of them. The Eastern church still does not use mechanical instruments in worship.

What can one woman do with her Sword? A retired Christian lady used her carport and a picnic table one summer to bring six neighborhood children together for a one-hour Bible Event Time each Saturday. She served each child a cookie and a drink at the end of each session.

Research and report on two simple ideas for educating children about Christianity.

_____

_____

~~~~~ HEAD IN THE SAND ~~~~~

We thank God for our freedoms each Sunday. Then we stand idly by and let those freedoms erode. We are on a tiny mound of sand in the midst of a worldly stream which daily takes chunks of freedom away. We must take our heads out of that eroding sand. You don't believe me? How many of our nation's children are being aborted?

We think Hitler was bad because he killed six million Jews, and Stalin ten million. But in the United States, since 1973, we have killed over fifty million babies!

WHAT CAN ONE WOMAN DO WITH HER SWORD?

You might say, "That is the world. It does not affect the church." I beg to differ. That silent shame does affect Christians. What if a young woman had an abortion and concealed it from the baby's father? In later years, if the abortion was confessed or discovered, it could cause a lot of agony, and even marital problems. Some women have negative emotional consequences for years after an abortion.

We are in a battle. We are being destroyed by our lack of Bible knowledge, our lack of a "thus saith the Lord" for everything. If you haven't noticed that, ask yourself how many Christians are divorcing.

Several years ago, my husband preached a sermon on marriage and divorce. A deacon made the statement from the pulpit that he had not heard a sermon on that subject in fifteen years. I was shocked. But think of the young people who have never heard a sermon on the subject. Fifteen years to them is a lifetime. I am happy that my husband presents a balance of topics from the pulpit. Preachers need to preach the whole counsel of God.

We do need good strong preachers, but even they usually bring us only two 30-minute sermons a week. One hour a week cannot supply Christian families with the Bible knowledge they must have.

How serious is abortion, the shedding of innocent blood? Fill in the blanks below and then discuss how Christians can take action on this issue.

"Manasseh shed very much _____ blood, till he had filled Jerusalem from one end to another, besides the sin that he made Judah to sin so that they did what was _____ in the sight of the Lord" (2 Kings 21:16).

"For he filled Jerusalem with _____ _____, and the Lord would _____ pardon" (2 Kings 24:4).

~ WALK AND TALK AND TEACH ~

I took responsibility for teaching my children at home. Our whole curriculum was based on God. The reason for our decision was a study of Daniel. But I emphasized Deuteronomy 6:6–7:

> And these words that I command you today shall be on your heart. You shall teach them diligently to your children, and shall talk of them when you sit in your house, and when you walk by the way, and when you lie down, and when you rise (Deuteronomy 6:6–7).

Incidental learning is informal learning that takes place without any intent to learn. Incidental learning requires neither research nor visible structure. The teacher deals with an incident and uses it to teach a truth. A godly parent uses it to teach godly truths. That is the best method for teaching children. The children and I often took hikes in the woods. As we observed trees and birds, we learned about our Creator. The children ran free along the bluffs of northwest Alabama. Richard loved the creek beds with their frogs, fish, and lizards. Later the children rode horses with their daddy.

Parental involvement and times of unstructured learning are some of the huge reasons homeschooling is so great. Preacher daddies are so immersed in their work that their kids sometimes feel neglected. Scott took time to be with our kids; the time was available because they were at home.

Fathers provide the sturdy framework for the home. They should be building a solid, dependable base for the family. Moms are more flexible. We kiss boo-boos, prepare meals, and work to stretch the family budget, whether the breadwinner is working or out of work, whether he is rich or poor, and whether times are good or bad. And God instructs fathers to bring their children up in the nurture and admonition of the Lord (Ephesians 6:4).

What is the "nurture of the Lord"? What is the "admonition of the Lord"?

List three ways parents can teach children in the family car while commuting to various events.

1. _____
2. _____
3. _____

LEAVE A LEGACY

So we are in a battle, and the Bible is to be wielded like a sword. How do we do that?

I am marking my Bible for my kids so when I am no longer with them, they will see what I thought about a verse. Do you wish to do that? If so, get a wide-margin Bible. Make a key on a blank page between the testaments and color code key words. *Forgiveness* in my Bible is blue and yellow. *Holy Spirit* is yellow and orange. Most sermons I hear get the color treatment. Also, I make my own chapters by ruling a line down the margin and inserting my own chapter heading. For example, outside James 1:13–15 is written, "How we are tempted."

When I hear a sermon about forgiveness, I put out to the side the next verse that is quoted, and at that verse I write the former verse. I am making my own chain reference. I also draw pictures in the margin. The wedding feast at Cana has large water jars in the margin. My Bible is my friend. It is dog-eared and worn. But when it is too full I will start on another. I also memorize scripture and rehearse these verses. Remember Jesus being tempted by the devil? How did the miracle worker, the express image of God, the creator-of-the-universe man, defeat the devil? He used scripture that He had memorized.

> And the tempter came and said to him, "If you are the Son of God, command these stones to become loaves of bread." But He answered, "It is written, 'Man shall not live by bread alone, but by every word that comes from the mouth of God'" (Matthew 4:3–4).

When is it most likely that Jesus learned scripture? He amazed the teachers in the temple with His understanding, so it is very likely that He learned scripture at Mary's knee (Luke 2:47).

Let's put on the whole armor of God, and, like Jesus, be ready to unsheathe the sword, because we are in a war with the tempter. Buckle up the belt of truth to hold that precious sword of faith, put on the breastplate of righteousness to protect your vital organs, and protect your feet with the gospel of peace so you can be ready to charge the enemy. Hold out that shield of faith to deflect the flaming darts of the evil one. Put on your helmet. Protect your mind with salvation. Wield that sword. Use it daily. It is your only offensive weapon. All your other gear is protective, so keep that sword sharp and at hand. It is the word of God (Hebrews 4:12). Exercise it.

Sweet sister, you are not in an army of one. You are in a battle alongside other precious Christians. Pray for them. Sometimes your sword will be needed to help the weak, and sometimes the weaker one is you. We need each other.

 **SHIPWRECK** During the time of my employment as a framer at Hobby Lobby, we were sometimes short staffed, so I worked as a cashier. There were no barcodes, and some of the specials were in "percentage off" bins. The sale price had to be manually calculated. I will never forget the day that a rather sophisticated lady brought an item to me.

"How much is this?"

I noted that the marked price was ten dollars and that it was from an eighty percent discount bin. "That is two dollars, ma'am," I replied.

"No, no," she argued. "That can't be right. It has to be more than that."

"No ma'am," I said gently. "That's what we're selling it for."

"Show me how you got that ridiculously low price," she quipped in a continuing argumentative tone.

As everyone who has worked in retail sales knows, the customer is always right, so I took out my hand-held calculator and did the simple operation: 10 x 80%. "See," I said. "You get eight dollars off. That leaves you owing two."

"Well, I never!" she muttered, half grinning. She was pleased, of course. After all, it was a rather good deal for her.

My daughter worked in a restaurant when she was 17. The supervisor asked an older girl to sweep the floor. The girl made repeated stabbing motions with the broom, as if she was trying to spear a fish. At age 19, she had never swept a floor.

Those examples of ignorance are sad, but the saddest thing in this world is the loss of the knowledge of God, our Creator.

When Jesus saw the masses leaving Him, He asked His disciples, "Do you want to go away as well?" But Simon Peter answered him, "Lord, to whom shall we go? You have the words of eternal life" (John 6:67–68).

James tells us life is a vapor (James 4:14), so our run on earth is short. Make every minute count for God so you and your children will be in heaven.

My dear friend Amy buried her son a few weeks ago. Nicholas was planning to serve God as a youth minister but was tragically killed in a tractor-trailer accident. His mother said, "I have no doubt where my son is now. He is in heaven with Jesus." That is the reason we need to know our Bible.

SHIP'S LOG

1. List some favorite scriptures that you have memorized. Share your findings with the class.

2. Tell the class how these verses have helped you.

3. What is the most pressing need of the church today? Share with the class.

CHAPTER FIVE

HARDSHIP
DEPRESSION'S GRIP

Have you ever been depressed? I have. I expended much effort trying to climb out of my dark tunnel. I could see the light at the end but I could never quite reach it on my own. I knew that God was out there, but I could not seem to get to Him. My counselor told me my condition was not caused by a lack of faith but by my inability to access the faith I had. He instructed me to write a journal. The writing helped me realize the cause of my depression. The couselor read the document, commended my efforts, and told me to burn it.

As smoke tendrils sent my woes skyward, I realized that some things were for God to resolve and not me. Was it my fault that I could not fix everything? For me, depression was a misplaced blame and guilt I had put on myself and also a misplaced belief that my love could solve issues that others did not want to acknowledge or to solve.

My mother imagined that I had a perfect life, but she and I had unresolved issues. I needed to forgive her for some matters and she needed to forgive me for others. But when two people are in conflict and one party does not recall the same things the other recalls, there is no basis for forgiveness. The offended party has to give those offenses to God and let go of bitterness.

~~~ WHATEVER! ~~~

At first I struggled even with turning to God. My mum had cancer. When she passed away, she and I were on opposite sides of the earth, ten thousand miles between us. Mum had never been willing to study the Bible with me, and every time I read and studied God's word, I felt overwhelmed with sadness for her.

Then I turned the matter over to God. He is the judge and I have no right to get into His business. He sees hearts and He knows all the burdens everyone has to bear. God understood my precious mummy and He understands me. Upon those conclusions I began my life's fascination and reliance on Paul's words to the Philippians:

> Let your reasonableness be known to everyone. The Lord is at hand; do not be anxious about anything, but in everything by prayer and supplication with thanksgiving let your requests be made known to God. And the peace of God, which surpasses all understanding, will guard your hearts and your minds in Christ Jesus. Finally, brothers, whatever is true, whatever is honorable, whatever is just, whatever is pure, whatever is lovely, whatever is commendable, if there is any excellence, if there is anything worthy of praise, think about these things. What you have learned and received and heard and seen in me—practice these things, and the God of peace will be with you (Philippians 4:5–9).

Whatever!

Whatever is honest, whatever is true;
Whatever I'm thinking controls what I do;
Whatever is just, whatever is pure,
Whatever my sin, heal my heart for its cure.
Whatever is lovely and good, Lord, I pray,
Get into my heart, from its throne guide my way.
If my heart can find virtue, O God, let me live it.
If someone is worthy of praise, let me give it.

Wherever the bend in my pathway may lead;
Whatever the struggle, whatever the need;
Whatever my heart, when it suffers or sings;
Whatever! O Lord, may I think on these things.

—Cindy Colley

How would your life be different if you gave your thoughts the "whatever" test of Philippians 4:8? Cross out thoughts in the list below that do not pass the test.

"Why is she so rude to me?"

"I need to repent."

"I'll never forgive him."

"I think she hates me."

"I know you'll do the right thing."

"Nobody can remember scripture like she does."

"This movie is 'R' but I'm mature."

"I can't help it if I have a bad temper."

Anxiety, worry, fear, and depression are negative thought habits. "For as he thinks in his heart so is he" (Proverbs 23:7 NKJV). How we think is how we are. If we think depressed, we are depressed.

NO FEAR

"For God has not given us the spirit of fear but of power and love and self-control" (2 Timothy 1:7). So if we have the spirit of fear, who gave it to us? The devil did! Remember, he is prowling around this earth seeking someone to devour, and his tastiest morsel, his favorite feast is the Christian. (See 1 Peter 5:8.) He has everyone else, so if he can tempt you with fear he will. But God is the giver of power and of a sound mind. Christ has defeated Satan. It took hardware—two planks and some nails—to make that perfect sacrifice. Satan bruised Christ's heel, but Satan suffered a death blow to the head when Jesus was crucified (Genesis 3:15). Hear the Hebrews writer:

> Since therefore the children share in flesh and blood, he himself likewise partook of the same things, that through death he might destroy the one who has the power of death, that is, the devil (Hebrews 2:14).

Satan, devil—*Satan* means "adversary." He is the deceiver that leads many astray. *Devil* means "slanderer." Someone who "casts through," making changes that destroy. He is a false accuser, unjustly criticizing to hurt and condemn. While "Satan" is used both in the Old and New Testament, "devil" is strictly a New Testament word.

Paul said, "Do not be anxious about anything" (Philippians 4:6). That is a command, so fear is not from God. Jesus said, "If you love me, you will keep my commandments" (John 14:15). My nana used to say, "Do not worry. Worry paralyzes action." Then she would add, "Don't worry, work!"

HEART GUARD

God's antidote for worry and anxiety is prayer with thanksgiving.

> But in everything by prayer and supplication with thanksgiving let your requests be made known to God (Philippians 4:6).

Write your feelings about how each phrase below can be a worry-buster:

"In everything"

"By prayer and supplication"

"With thanksgiving"

Have you ever taken a problem to God and begun that prayer by thanking Him for the many blessings He was already giving you? When even the breath we breathe is a gift from a powerful loving God, we should be so much more thankful. When we begin to realize the truth of His goodness, our anxiety begins to ebb. That is because we know that the God who created the universe and cares for us will handle it.

> And the peace of God, which surpasses all understanding, will guard your hearts and your minds in Christ Jesus (Philippians 4:7).

We are in a battle. Satan truly is after our minds. But remember that the mind of God's woman is protected, hedged about, and guarded (Job 1:10; Psalm 139:5). Her mind is protected because she is living safely in Christ Jesus. Satan cannot get to her mind if she constantly buffers it with daily prayers of thankfulness.

～～～ WHATEVER IS REAL ～～～

If you are depressed, you are habitually depositing negative thoughts into your brain's bank. Have you ever lain in bed thinking, "What is the point in getting up?" or "Why make the bed?" Depression makes you feel lifeless, which leads to doubts and worries. If you feel like that, these words are for you: "Finally, brothers, whatever is true . . . " (Philippians 4:8). That means whatever is real. You have been in the habit of focusing on worry, doubt, and fear. Ask yourself, "How much of what I am worrying about is real?"

So as you lie there, retrain your mind. Focus on what is real and not what is imagined. The reality is that God loves you. Think on that. Then think about Christ's love for you, love that He has proved many times over. And God wants you to love yourself.

"For the whole law is fulfilled in one word: 'You shall love your neighbor as yourself'" (Galatians 5:14). We are commanded to love others as we love ourselves. Think about that as you change your mind's bad habits. Then make a habit of thinking wholesome, godly, and wonderful things. With those things, you will replace doubt and fear, the antitheses of faith.

"For the weapons of our warfare are not of the flesh but have divine power to destroy strongholds. We destroy arguments and every lofty opinion raised against the _____ of God, and take every _____ captive to obey Christ" (2 Corinthians 10:4–5).

What is the meaning of the above verse? How can it help us to change our thinking habits?

_____

_____

HEART TREASURE

Put God's word into your mind. Rehearse His loving advice for you as you go about your day. Our thinking, more than anything else, forms our character. Jesus said,

> The good person out of the good treasure of his heart produces good, and the evil person out of his evil treasure produces evil, for out of the abundance of the heart his mouth speaks (Luke 6:45).

Put good treasure into your mind's bank by studying God's word.

"Do not lay up for yourselves _____ on
earth, where moth and rust destroy and where thieves break
in and steal, but lay up for yourselves _____
in _____, where neither moth nor rust destroys
and where thieves do not break in and steal. For where your
_____ is, there your _____ will be
also" (Matthew 6:19–21).

DON'T RUN ON EMPTY

When I was an 18-year-old college student, I learned the gospel and put my Lord on in baptism (Galatians 3:27). In the summer after, I worked as a painter, painting houses at a historic museum. My coworkers continually used foul language. As a new Christian, I was trying hard to give that up. But the more I thought about not swearing, the more swear words crept into my mind. Oh! How the devil loves the tender young shoot that is a new Christian. I am glad a wise woman told me to replace the bad thoughts with Bible verses.

Jesus taught that biblical principle:

"When the unclean spirit has gone out of a person, it passes
through waterless places seeking rest, and finding none it
says, "I will return to my house from which I came." And
when it comes, it finds the house _____ and put in
_____. Then it goes and brings seven other spirits
more evil than itself, and they enter and _____
there. And the last state of that person is _____
than the first" (Luke 11:24–26).

In this illustration from Luke 11, think of your mind as the house. Think of my trying not to swear, but as I left my mind empty, more and more swear words crowded into my thoughts. Then I began the habit of replacing each bad word with a memory verse like, "I can do all things through him who strengthens me" (Philippians 4:13) or "Trust in the Lord with all your heart, and do not lean on your own understanding. In all your ways acknowledge him, and he will make straight your paths" (Proverbs 3:5–6).

One day at school I was running down a path. As I was passing an open metal window, I slipped on the hard, wet ground. The window gouged my neck and broke my fall. I lay there in the rain for a moment. When I slowly rose to my feet, I saw some of my neighbors poking their heads out their windows to see what had happened. I began punching my fists into the air yelling, "Eureka, I did it!" I did it because, instead of swearing, I had said, "Crumbs!" All my efforts to put good thoughts in to replace the bad had worked!

Define the "whatevers" of Philippians 4:8 in your own words:

True _____

Honorable _____

Just _____

Pure _____

Lovely _____

Commendable _____

Excellent _____

Praiseworthy _____

If we want our battle with hardships of depression and negative thinking to be successful, we should focus on Philippians 4:8 and change our thinking to concentrate on what is real. Focus on the truths that God loves you and Jesus loves you. Heaven is real, and we can study God's word to help us get there.

Next, focus on thankfulness. Rehearse your blessings in prayer to God (Philippians 4:6). Defeat negative and depressed thoughts by concentrating on positive godly ones. We cannot be anxious and negative while we are thanking God for our blessings. It is biblical: we are what we think. And our wonderful Father has given us, not a spirit of fear, but one of a sound mind.

Your thinking determines who you are, and you control that.

Shipwreck! Just to pronounce the word sends chills down the spine of anyone who has been on the seas—maybe even those who have been in a small boat on a big river. What happens when you wreck your ship? Only those who are prepared and skilled have hope of surviving such a maritime disaster.

Think of Judas Iscariot. He was not prepared for the enormity of the wreck he created when he marched into the quarters of the chief priest to begin negotiations to hand Jesus over to the temple authorities: "What are you willing to give me if I deliver him over to you?" After all the time Judas had spent with the Master, he had failed to retrain his thinking. He had not learned to meditate on what was true, what was noble, or what was of good report. If so, he would have received forgiveness of his egregious sin from our loving, merciful God.

Then when Judas, his betrayer, saw that Jesus was condemned, he changed his mind and brought back the thirty pieces of silver to the chief priests and the elders, saying, "I have sinned by betraying innocent blood." They said, "What is that to us? See to it yourself." And throwing down the pieces of silver into the temple, he departed, and he went and hanged himself (Matthew 27:3–5).

Now consider Peter. Long before sunrise on that cold spring morning, Peter warmed himself by the fire, listening intently to the "not going so well" court preceedings. "You also were with Jesus the Galilean" (Matthew 26:69). The words of a servant girl shocked him into reality. "I do not know what you mean" (v. 70). That violent lie seemed to spew without thought from his lips. Why? Because Satan was sitting astride the throne in Peter's heart, directing the affairs of Jesus' servant. And Satan didn't let Peter stop there. A second time Peter denied his Lord. Then with the third denial, he invoked a curse on himself and swore that he did not know Jesus (v. 74).

But you know the rest of the story. Peter became a great apostle because, unlike Judas, he expelled Satan, abandoned his foundering vessel, and found safety in his Lord.

Do not make shipwreck of your faith when faced with hardship. Dig deep and hold fast to the principles of Philippians 4:8. Then hold fast to God and all His word.

SHIP'S LOG

1. Make a list of verses that you can use to replace negativity. Share these with the class.

2. Name some ways that you are laying up treasures in heaven.

3. To help retrain your thinking, write the acrostic F.O.C.U.S. at the top of a page each day. It means Follow One Course Until Successful. This will help you take baby steps. It has been said that to form a habit you must do a thing fifteen times in succession. Renew your mind, change a bad habit by F.O.C.U.S. Share your success with the class.

CHAPTER SIX

DICTATORSHIP
"MY WAY OR THE HIGHWAY" WOMEN

You know the phrase, "If Momma ain't happy, then nobody's happy." Some women think that phrase is scripture. Well, it ain't. In my experience it should read, "If Daddy ain't happy, then nobody's happy."

Happiness is something people have to decide within themselves. I knew a woman who was divorcing her husband because he no longer made her happy. In reality, she was choosing not to be pleased with him. We have it backwards if we think our husbands should make us happy. That is not their job!

Happiness does not depend on another person, so do not try to give anyone that power over you. Happiness resides with self and with God. No one makes anyone else happy; that is up to you. It is your choice. That is why some who have had very bad things happen to them still have a beautiful smile and a jubilant attitude. We cannot change the many trials that happen to us, but we can change our attitudes concerning those catastrophes.

⚓ "The wisest of women builds her house, but folly with her own hands tears it down" (Proverbs 14:1).

✵ "An excellent wife is the crown of her husband, but she who brings shame is like rottenness in his bones" (Proverbs 12:4).

A SUITABLE HELPER

Remember how our Creator made us, and why we were made. "There was not found a helper fit for him" (Genesis 2:20). Adam's job was to name all the animals. As they gathered around him in pairs, it must have dawned on him that he had no one.

Great happiness often comes after great sacrifice and doing without. Adam was alone. Each animal enjoyed companionship, but not Adam.

If you get everything you want at the snap of your fingers, you don't enjoy those things as much as the poor person who receives a small blessing. In late summer 2005, my daughter went with a school group to help victims in the aftermath of Hurricane Katrina. When she gave a small inexpensive pillow to a little boy, he jumped up and down with joy. His reaction both amazed and humbled her.

Can you imagine Adam's joy when he awoke from a divinely induced sleep and saw the most beautiful creature he had ever beheld? Was his joy greater because he had been alone? Of course it was. The lesson Adam then learned was that God supplies needs, because God created her from Adam's rib: "The man called his wife's name Eve, because she was the mother of all living" (Genesis 3:20).

MARRIAGE SCENES

Let us now consider a young couple in today's society, and let's call them Adam and Eve. Eve has a degree. She works in a fancy office downtown, quite a distance from the hospital where Adam works. Eve's career is very important to her. No kids are going to tie her down! With a pop-tart in one hand and a Styrofoam cup of coffee in the other, Adam and Eve peck each other on the cheek each morning as they part company.

And yes, the kids do come along, so Adam takes them to day-care one morning, Eve the next. After work they rendezvous at a restaurant before picking up the kids. Then the selected parent drives to daycare while the other arrives first at their massive mort-gaged-to-the-hilt suburban mansion and begins to prepare for the next day.

Over time, a wedge develops between them, small at first but it begins to swell as stress increases. Eventually, and almost inevitably, an irreparable split is staring them both in the face. They opt for the permanent "fix." Then divorced, beaten up, and emotionally bruised, each suffers alone during the week. On weekends the one who doesn't have the children hangs out at a favorite nightspot, attempting to bring joy into a life that wouldn't recognize joy if it met her on the street in broad daylight. How often is this scenario played out in our society?

God's plan is different and far more beautiful. Here it is. She leaves her mother and father and joins him. He leaves his family and cleaves to her. Her desire is for her husband, and he takes the head-ship and authority in the marriage. Yes, that is right!

God said to the first woman, "Your _____ shall be for your _____, and he shall _____ over you" (Genesis 3:16).

Which word in one of the blanks above is too difficult for women to understand? Why?

_____

_____

Observe at least three married couples this week. How does the woman convey her "desire"? Why do women tend to focus their desire on children or career instead of on their husbands?

_____

_____

My dear sister, God Almighty determined leadership in the home. No, the husband is not more important than his wife, but leadership is his role. How does he do it? Paul explained it this way: "Husbands, love your wives, as Christ also loved the church and gave himself up for her" (Ephesians 5:25).

Peter says, "Husbands, live with your wives in an understanding way, showing honor to the woman as the weaker vessel" (1 Peter 3:7). Sometimes we just run over that word *honor*. In 1 Timothy 1:17, that same word is used of worship to God. It means "to pay respect, to place a value on, the value willingly assigned to something." God is emphasizing that a wife is to hold a position of high esteem in her husband's life.

Husbands have an even more specific command. They are to love us as Jesus loved the church, to love us even enough to die for us. I am more than willing to submit to a man like that. There is nothing sexier than knowing your man would die for you. In fact, like Jesus, he is to die to the world, to the ways of the world, and to nurture his home as Jesus does His church. The Christian husband will listen to his wife as an equal, and his decisions will always be made with her input in mind.

God fashioned a perfect helper for Adam. She fit! However, Paul said in 1 Corinthians 7:7–8, "I wish all were as I myself am . . . To the _____ and the widows I say that it is good for them to _____ single as I am." Compare Genesis 2:18: "It is not good that man should be alone." Discuss.

Research how men view the "suitable" or "fit" helper. Compare those qualifications with those taught in scripture.

_____

_____

~~~~~ CONFUSE THE COOK ~~~~~

Laughing at potentially explosive situations is a good way to safely let off steam. There have been times when that piece of information has helped me out of a hot spot when things didn't go right in the kitchen. You know how it is to begin to prepare a meal only to remember you missed all the Thursday specials at the supermarket because of a dental appointment. Then the Friday dinner needs a lot of extra help. On one of those occasions, I became rather creative—chicken and dumplings from scratch. All was going well until, right in the middle of that important task, Scott notified me that he was running late for dinner—sixty-four minutes late, as it turned out! My fluffy dumplings got heavier and heavier until, at the point of no return, they morphed into a sodden, gluey mess.

Our family gathered for the meal. Scott looked down at the bowl, looked up at me and the kids and said, "I can't pray thanks to God for this!"

There was a pause and we all began to laugh. Instead of yelling at him for keeping us waiting an hour, we laughed and headed for McDonald's.

My biscuit making skills were also awful. You should never have to gnaw a biscuit with your back molars. Scott told the kids that the South would have won the Civil War with them. They could have been used in the cannons!

I have a friend who said, "Such comments about my cooking would make me cry!" My attitude is that a few badly cooked meals ensure that we eat out occasionally.

~~~~~ CREATIVE DISCIPLINE ~~~~~

A sunny disposition helped me raise my kids, but the threat to embarrass them was my favorite and best weapon. My girls were growing up when belly button piercing was the rage. Many of their friends were rolling pants down and shirts up to reveal as much stomach as possible. My rule with our kids was simple: "If I see skin I will blow a raspberry on it no matter where you are." Needless to say, their shirts covered any chance of skin show-off!

Also it did my heart good when I went shopping for summer clothes and my youngest looked at the shortest shorts. You know the ones where the pockets are longer than the frayed shorts are? She quickly announced she would only wear capris. That was her decision. She surely didn't want me blowing raspberries on all that skin.

Clothes shopping also earned me kudos from my husband. He once took the girls to buy skirts. Enough time passed that I began to worry. At last Scott burst through the door, headed for the recliner, and flopped into it exhausted. Then he asked, "How do you do it?" The girls had to have the right fabric, the right length, the right brand. The whole ordeal was exhausting, plus it took hours to find a modest skirt. "That's a good problem for a daddy with two beautiful girls," I reminded him.

~~~ ROLL WITH YOUR ROLE ~~~

The wise woman builds her house. The best way for us to do that is to have a clear idea of women's role in the marriage. The husband is the wife's desire, and children are the primary responsibility of both husband and wife. Let's make it a priority to spend quality Bible time with our children.

How much time do we spend chasing urgent trivialities—ball games and school events and music lessons, whatever!—and how little time with activities of eternal values that enrich their souls? How much time are you investing in teaching the Bible to your children? Immerse yourself and them in God's word.

Homeschooling was a great blessing to us. The children saw God's hand in everything. When we couldn't afford lessons they needed, our answered prayers made God real to them. When problems arose, we opened the Bible and found what God thought on the subject. He became real to them.

Parents must be their kids' mentors, not their peers. They must present a united front to their children. Never compete with your husband for your children's affection. You are a team, not competitors. Be the parent, not the buddy. Love, discipline, and train your children. Friendship will come later when the children are grown. Laugh a lot in your home.

Be the parent, not the buddy.

As Christians, we must change the saying from "If Momma ain't happy, then nobody's happy," to "If God ain't happy, then nobody's happy."

Each year I pray a prayer daily from the scriptures. One year I prayed from Genesis 3:16. Every day I asked God for my desire to be for Scott. Isn't it remarkable how God answers daily prayer? I hear you ask, "But isn't that vain repetition?" My thinking on that is if I pray pure scripture, then God will be pleased. It actively directed me to look for the good in my husband. You truly see the positive qualities when you look for them.

Married women, supply answers below with your own personal prayer from Genesis 3:16:

Heavenly Father, Please help my _____ to be for my husband _____ —and help him to rule over _____.

What consequence might develop when a wife competes with her husband for the children's affection?

_____

_____

Why is it unwise to try to be a buddy rather than a parent? Support your answer with scripture.

_____

_____

How can strife be diverted by a good sense of humor? Give your own example.

_____

_____

What Bible verse promotes laughter?

_____

~~~~~ FAMILY BIBLE TIME ~~~~~

My son's two precious boys are three and one. Every night they have a family devotional with Bible songs, Bible reading, and prayer. The boys are asked, "What was your favorite thing today?" Three-year-old Gabriel often answers, "Our family devo!" He loves snuggling with his daddy and mommy and appreciates that they are both focused on him, his brother, and God. He is often heard to say, "I love my family." He means his whole family, because occasionally Granny and Granddaddy are there at family devotional time, thanks to Skype.

Use your church library resources or google "family Bible time" to search for material that is age-appropriate for your kids. Arrange a "moms and grandmothers get-together" for the specific purpose of brainstorming on this topic. Encourage each participant to consider a "resource space" in her home where outgrown material can be recycled. List some of your ideas.

_____

_____

_____

~~~~ LOVE MUCH, DICTATE LESS ~~~~

Remember, "Do not withhold good from those to whom it is due, when it is in your power to do it" (Proverbs 3:27).

Do not demand of those around you: "Do my bidding! Make me happy!" That mind-set will only make you feel empty and hollow, because you know you are holding hostage everyone you love. Instead, look to fulfill their needs. Never withhold good from your loved ones. If you have to admit that you treat strangers better than you treat your husband and kids, get over yourself, and step off that train going nowhere.

Pick your battle. Stand up for the true desires of your heart. Do not sweat the small stuff. Enjoy your family and kids. Never insist on your way if it isn't God's way. But do, if it is. Remember, when Sarah told Abraham to "cast out the bondwoman," God told Abraham that Sarah was right and that he should listen to her (Genesis 21:12).

And remember, love covers a multitude of sins. Love much; dictate less.

We avoid contentious people, so refuse to be the foolish woman who tears down her home. If you insist on being a constant drip, drip, drip mom or wife, your family will escape from your presence. When you find them, they will be huddled together on the proverbial rooftop, trying to comfort one another. Release your firm grasp! Resolve to be the godly woman who builds up. Let God take over and enjoy the ride!

Midwife—"Midwife" is from Middle English *midwif*, which means "with woman (*mid*, 'with'; *wif*, 'woman'). a person (typically a woman) trained to assist women in childbirth.

 **SHIPWRECK** The first fourteen chapters of Exodus give the readers a front-row-seat view of a true dictator venting his domination and cruelty upon his slaves. Pharaoh had risen to power and wealth on the backs of the Hebrews who built many of the massive buildings and statuary surrounding him. His

slaves were obviously a threat to the status quo, so he could not allow them to continue to increase in power and threaten national security. In an effort to assure Egypt's safety he commanded that all the males born to Hebrew women be killed at birth. When the Hebrew mid-wives refused to accommodate him, Pha-raoh commanded all his people, "Every son that is born to the Hebrews you shall cast into the Nile, but you shall let every daughter live" (Exodus 1:22).

Pharaoh's flagrant disregard for human life and his cruel oppression reminds me of two mass murderers of the twentieth century—Germany's Adolf Hitler and the Soviet Union's Joseph Stalin. Stalin even killed most members of his family. Dictators think they have ultimate con-trol by the strength of their military, but the power of the God of heaven is infinitely greater. The ten plagues He sent on Pharaoh were proof of that.

Don't cling to your "baby"—the six-foot-two university freshman.

It fascinates me that in Egyptian history there was a pharaoh called Thutmoses, the date of whose reign coincided with that of the exodus of the Israelites from Egypt. Pharaoh's daughter, Hapshepsut, might have been the princess who rescued Jochebed's baby from the river. Whoever the princess was who saved that Hebrew child, we know she called him "Drawn," for she drew him out of the water. The Hebrews translated his name into their language as "Moses."

Let's remember Pharaoh, whose hard heart caused him to play a military game called "Dictator Shipwreck." We must learn from him that as life progresses things we control move beyond our reach. When we determine to cling unrelentingly to our "baby"—that six-foot-two university freshman—not only are we going to run our own vessel aground, but we are also going to torpedo his ship.

SHIP'S LOG

1. Resolve to be a better wife this week. Actively decide to do something special for your husband each day.

2. Resolve to be better to your kids by truly listening to them. Set aside a gadget-free time each day. If you haven't already established entertainment-free zones, make the dining table a place where the family can relax, eat, and enjoy casual conversation.

CHAPTER SEVEN

WORSHIP
GOD AND ME

I taught my children grammar by teaching them what questions to ask. For example, to find an adjective you must ask, Which one? What kind? How many? To find an adverb you ask, How? When? Where? So we can instantly see that "quickly" is an adverb, and so is "yesterday." So let's ask some questions concerning worship. Why? Who? How? What? When? Where?

WHY DO WE WORSHIP?

The answer is simple: God has put eternity in our hearts (Ecclesiastes 3:11). We were created with a sense of God within us and a desire to reach out to Him (Acts 17:27). As a result we seek to bow before Him, to pay homage to Him, to worship Him.

The Genesis account shows us that man is very different from the animals. God breathed into Adam's nostrils the breath of life, and he became a living soul (Genesis 2:7). No animal received God-breathed CPR. Man did. No animal has an eternal soul. Man does. So we worship because we were designed that way.

The first example of worship is recorded in Genesis.

> In the course of time Cain brought to the Lord an offering of the fruit of the ground, and Abel also brought of the firstborn of his

flock and of their fat portions. And the Lord had regard for Abel and his offering, but for Cain and his offering he had no regard (Genesis 4:3–5).

Abel's offering showed true sacrifice, because it was the best he had to offer. Two verses in the New Testament shed light on Abel's superior offering. Hebrews 11:4 says, "By faith Abel offered to God a more acceptable sacrifice than Cain." Add to this the words of Paul, "So faith comes from hearing, and hearing through the word of Christ" (Romans 10:17). Both Abel and Cain heard God, and Abel obeyed. Worship that pleases God demands sacrifice of our best. When we toss the leftovers from our pockets into the Sunday morning collection plate and slouch in the pew while doing so, we are acting as Cain did. Our giving to God must be our first priority, for was that not His priority in giving us Jesus? Write that check first, before you divide your money to pay bills.

> I know not what Christ will say to you in the great day. I fear there are many who may know well that they are not Christians because they do not love to give. To give largely and liberally, not grudgingly at all, requires a new heart; an old heart would rather part with its life-blood than its money. Oh, my friends! Enjoy your money; make the most of it; give none away; enjoy it quickly for I can tell you, you will be beggars throughout eternity.
>
> —Robert Murray M'Cheyne

"When you offer blind animals in sacrifice, is that not _____? And when you offer those that are lame or sick, is that not _____? Present that to your governor; will he _____ you or show you favor? says the _____ of hosts" (Malachi 1:8).

How do our poor contribution excuses that we label as "forgetful" or "busy" compare with the word God chose to describe leftovers?

_____

_____

The Laodiceans thought they had everything. Read Revelation 3:15–18 and discuss God's view of their possessions. Comment on the possibility of their giving "as prospered." Why does self-sufficiency often lead to lukewarmness?

_____

_____

～～ THE "WHO" OF WORSHIP ～～

Who do we worship? Not family, not self, not the almighty dollar. God! We must worship the Lord in His beauty (Psalms 95:6) and God our Creator (Genesis 1:1) and God, the incorruptible (Romans 1:22–23). We must worship the Maker, not the made!

> **Worship**—Reverent honor and homage paid to God or a sacred personage, or to any object regarded as sacred; to render religious reverence and homage; to feel an adoring reverence or regard for any person or thing.

Romans 1:25: "They exchanged the _____ about God for a _____ and _____ and _____ the _____ rather than the Creator."

Read the context in verses 21–25 and list at least six characteristics of the unrighteous.

1. _____   4. _____

2. _____   5. _____

3. _____   6. _____

Select two false gods and research methods of worship to them—Baal, Buddha, Wiccan deities, Hindu deities, others of your choice.

Contrast one specific characteristic of four false gods with one characteristic of Jehovah.

False God	Jehovah

～～ HOW DO WE WORSHIP? ～～

We must worship obediently as Abel did. And as Abraham did when he offered Isaac, we must give according to God's demands (Genesis 22:1–18).

Describe the different approaches to God in the Patriarchal, Mosaical, and Christian Age.

_____

_____

_____

Find at least two Bible texts that show us we must worship obediently. Then find two scriptures that demonstrate disobedient worship.

Obedient Worship	Disobedient Worship

An attitude of obedience involves "Thy will be done" just as our Savior taught His disciples to pray. Shouldn't we worship prayerfully? The following prayer should be ours as we enter worship:

Incline your ear, O Lord, and answer me,
　　for I am poor and needy.
Preserve my life, for I am godly;
　　save your servant, who trusts in you—you are my God.
Be gracious to me, O Lord,
　　for to you do I cry all the day.
Gladden the soul of your servant,
　　for to you, O Lord, do I lift up my soul.
For you, O Lord, are good and forgiving,
　　abounding in steadfast love to all who call upon you.

—Psalm 86:1–5

WHAT ARE WE TO DO
IN WORSHIP?

Because of our desire to please God, we want to do just as Jesus and
His apostles did.

⚙ *They sang, so we sing* (Colossians 3:16).

Jesus promised He would sing with us. Find that scripture
in Hebrews, and write it here.

_____

Consider the controversy in the religious world around
music in worship. Why is singing often *not* considered to
be music?

_____

Instruments of music were an integral part of Old
Testament worship, but where is the mention of
instruments in the law of Christ? Find three scriptures
that tell us about the music and the purpose of it in the
Christian's worship. Circle the one that mentions using an
instrument.

1. _____

2. _____

3. _____

⚙ *They prayed, so we pray* (Acts 2:42).

Early Christians continued "steadfastly" in prayer. Jesus ear-
lier taught His disciples to pray concisely and specifically (Matthew 6:9–13). Examples of specific prayers are found throughout
the Bible. Abraham's servant Eliezer prayed in grateful worship

after he prayed specifically for success in his mission to find an appropriate wife for Isaac. Read about this touching romantic scene in Genesis 24.

How can we determine God's providence in our lives if we pray too generally, such as "for the sick, the world over"? Eliezer's prayer was specific, and God answered him. Rebekah watered his ten camels, exactly as he requested of God! No small task for Rebekah, either; a camel can drink twenty gallons at a single visit to the watering trough!

Then after Rebekah had finished her self-appointed task, Abraham's servant Eliezer worshiped the Lord in prayer:

> Blessed be the Lord, the God of my master Abraham, who has not forsaken his steadfast love and his faithfulness toward my master (Genesis 24:27).

We too should offer a prayer of thanksgiving when we receive our answer to prayer. When we pray for the sick ones in our congregations and they recover, we should then thank God for His mercy.

Regularly thank the Lord for His provision. Thank Him for everything! In Luke 17, Jesus healed ten lepers. Only one of them returned to acknowledge Jesus' deed, and he was a Samaritan, believe it or not! And that Samaritan did not simply say, "Thank you," but he fell at Jesus' feet in adoration to thank Him. Leprosy was a horrible disease, but we have been cured of far worse. Jesus has cured us from sin and delivered us from eternal condemnation, so we must be the most thankful people on earth! (Romans 8:1–2).

We worship God through Jesus, so each prayer should be in His name (John 14:13–14).

DO WE PRAY TOO GENERALLY . . . "THE SICK, THE WORLD OVER"?

And whatever you do, in word or deed, do everything in the _____ of the _____ _____, giving _____ to God the Father through him (Colossians 3:17).

Rejoice always, _____ without ceasing, give _____ in all circumstances; for this is the will of God in Christ Jesus for you (1 Thessalonians 5:16–18).

Circle the correct answer:

The scriptures above are (1) suggestions. (2) commands.

✸ *They gave, so we give* (1 Corinthians 16:1–2).

The churches of Galatia and Corinth were directed to have a collection every week.

"On the first day of _____ week, each of you is to put something aside and store it up, as he may _____, so that there will be no collecting when I come" (1 Corinthians 16:2).

What is the wisdom in a weekly collection?

_____

If the church meets four times weekly, is there to be a collection at every meeting? _____

How much were the early Christians commanded to give?

_____

From your Bible, find the answers to the following questions in 2 Corinthians 8:1–5:

1. What phrases describe the Macedonian churches?

   _____

2. What phrases describe how they gave?

   _____

3. What verse shows that their attitude was not one of duty?

   _____

4. What phrase describes their priority?

   _____

We have already discussed giving God leftovers. The questions you just answered reinforce the concept of giving God your best. How much does He want? He wants all of you.

�֍ *They observed the Lord's supper, so we observe the Lord's supper* (1 Corinthians 11:23–26).

When we come together on the first day of every week, we also worship the Lord by remembering His death and resurrection in the Lord's supper:

> For I received from the Lord what I also delivered to you, that the Lord Jesus on the night when he was betrayed took bread, and when he had given thanks, he broke it, and said, "This is my body which is for you. Do this in remembrance of me." In the same way also he took the cup, after supper, saying, "This cup is the new covenant in my blood. Do this, as often as you drink it, in remembrance of me." For as often

as you eat this bread and drink the cup, you proclaim the Lord's death until he comes.

What does it mean to take the Lord's supper in an "unworthy manner"? How serious is this infraction? Clarify the phrase "discerning the Lord's body" (1 Corinthians 11:27–29).

Acts 20:7 says the disciples met to "break bread." In the Bible, "break bread" sometimes refers to eating a common meal. To what else does it refer? When it does not refer to a common meal, on what day of the week was it observed?

～～～ WHEN DO WE WORSHIP? ～～～

We should be submissive to God always. Paul said, "Pray without ceasing" (1 Thessalonians 5:17), so is the church always assembled? Our assembly for worship might be at any time, but our example for a special and mandated assembly is on the first day of the week. The church began on the first day of the week. Jesus was resurrected on the first day of the week. The church gave on the first day of the week. The church participated in the Lord's supper on the first day of the week. Historically, the New Testament church met for worship on the first day of every week. The first day, Sunday, is the day all Christians are appointed to gather for worship.

~~~ WHERE DO WE WORSHIP? ~~~

The Samaritan woman at the well conversed with Jesus about this question. "Our fathers worshiped on this mountain, but you say that in Jerusalem is the place where people ought to worship" (John 4:20).

Jesus responded, "The hour is coming when neither on this mountain nor in Jerusalem will you worship the Father" (John 4:21). He then explained to her what God was looking for in worship, and what true worshipers must do to please Him.

> But the hour is coming, and is now here, when the true worshipers will worship the Father in spirit and truth, for the Father is seeking such people to worship Him. God is spirit, and those who worship Him must worship in spirit and truth (John 4:23–24).

In Jesus' day, it was important for the Jews to worship in Jerusalem, but now the emphasis of worship is not on the place but on the heart. Jesus changed the "where" of worship from geography to "heart-ography." God now requires a right attitude (spirit) and a right pattern (truth) for our worship to be acceptable.

Reflect on the simplicity of Christian worship. Draw a contrast between worship under the law of Moses and worship under the law of Christ.

Moses' Law	Christ's Law
Feasts and Holy Days	
Sacrifices and Tithes	
Trumpets and Cymbals	
Prayers by Priests	
Other	

What a pleasure it is to "enter his gates with thanksgiving, and his courts with praise!" (Psalm 100:4). As a child, I can recall my intense search for God. As a young mother, I can recall preparing my little children on Saturday evenings for the great event that was to come the next day.

To worship God the way the church of the New Testament worshiped is a joy unspeakable. Plan your life around worshiping God, not your worship around your life. It is a joyful and thankful expression to acknowledge the greatness of God.

> Yet you do not know what tomorrow will bring. What is your life? For you are a mist that appears for a little time and then vanishes. Instead you ought to say, "If the Lord wills, we will live and do this or that." As it is, you boast in your arrogance. All such boasting is evil. So whoever knows the right thing to do and fails to do it, for him it is sin (James 4:14–17).

> Simon Peter answered him, "Lord, to whom shall we go? You have the words of eternal life" (John 6:68).

If we devise worship in our own hearts as Jeroboam did, we will not have eternal life but everlasting punishment. Yikes! We who are vapor must get this right!

Worship is not a burden but a privilege. When I reach my hands to toddler granddaughter Emma, via technology, and sing "Jesus Loves Me," that is a delight. What a joy it is to worship the Lord.

I was glad when they said to me,
"Let us go to the house of the Lord!"
—Psalm 122:1

SHIPWRECK

We just had worship, sitting right here in our living room, with our one-year-old granddaughter in her mother's arms in Singapore. What a precious time they set aside every night before bed, and what a delight for us to sing "Jesus Loves Me" with them via Skype.

What if we forgot God, as Jeroboam did? He built temples on high places and appointed priests from among all the people, instead of following God's plan for Aaron's descendents to be priests. He further devised a plan to worship according to the ways of the Egyptians by making two golden calves as Aaron did at Mount Sinai (Exodus 32:4). Jeroboam had a different motive but he committed the same sin: "You have gone up to Jerusalem long enough. Behold your gods, O Israel, who brought you up out of the land of Egypt" (1 Kings 12:28).

> *P*LAN LIFE AROUND WORSHIP, NOT WORSHIP AROUND LIFE.

With great confidence he set up one at Dan in the northern part of his kingdom and the other at Bethel near the southern border, only a few miles north of Jerusalem. Now his constituents had no excuse for going to Jerusalem where they might be tempted to pledge their allegiance to Rehoboam, king of the southern kingdom.

Jeroboam went up to the altar that he had made in Bethel on the fifteenth day of the eighth month. He devised that date in his own heart, not by God's authority. God had instituted the Feast of Tabernacles for the fifteenth day of the month of Tishri. That was the seventh month, not the eighth. But Jeroboam believed he was in charge, so he did what he thought was best for himself politically (1 Kings 12:33).

Jeroboam's initial acts plunged Israel into a downward spiral from which they would not recover. God could not have been more displeased. Why do we sometimes act as Jeroboam did and devise plans in our hearts and forget God? Eternal life is at stake!

SHIP'S LOG

1. Discuss our worship in giving in light of Malachi 3:8–10.

2. How can we each make our worship more meaningful?

3. How can we better teach our children to worship?

CHAPTER EIGHT

COURTSHIP
WORTHY WOMEN FIRST

God's beautiful plan for courtship and marriage should be according to Proverbs 31 instead of "Uh oh, I've been caught-ship!"

When we are looking for that special someone, we can completely overlook the fact that we are to be someone else's special someone. Instead of hunting for some guy and being miserable about not finding him, concentrate on yourself instead.

Become a "more precious than jewels" woman.

> An excellent wife who can find? She is far more precious than jewels. The heart of her husband trusts in her, and he will have no lack of gain. She does him good, and not harm, all the days of her life (Proverbs 31:10–12).

This means that you must acknowledge that you are truly precious and valuable. Often because of a failure to love self, we attract the wrong kind of man. Instead, look in the mirror and say, "God loves me, Jesus loves me, the Holy Spirit loves me, and I love me. I will not put up with disrespect, neglect, or abuse. I am precious, far more precious than jewels. I want someone to cherish the woman I am and be the one who will help me get to heaven."

What, if any, are the dangers of concentrating totally on what I want instead of what others want? Support your answer with scripture.

_____

_____

_____

JEWELS FROM
THE ROYAL LAW

The Proverbs 31 woman loved herself. She followed the royal law of James 2:8: "If you really fulfill the royal law according to the scripture, 'You shall love your neighbor as yourself,' you are doing well."

If you do not first love yourself, how can you hope to love others? Also, you want to be a person who can be trusted as you continue your courtship. I asked a friend whose husband had Huntington's disease how she was coping with his change in personality. She said, "Because I trust and respect him, I can cope." For her, love was built on trust and respect. That is the bedrock of life-lasting love. The passion and romance of a giddy whirlwind fling are temporary. Feelings are transient. Build your marriage on the love of 1 Corinthians 13. In fact, put your name where love is, and his name will also be there. That will immediately show you if his love will last throughout a lifelong marriage.

> Love is patient and kind; love does not envy or boast; it is not arrogant or rude. It does not insist on its own way; it is not irritable or resentful; it does not rejoice at wrongdoing, but rejoices with the truth. Love bears all things, believes all things, hopes all things, endures all things. Love never ends. As for prophecies, they will pass away; as for tongues, they will cease; as for knowledge, it will pass away. For we know in part and we prophesy

in part, but when the perfect comes, the partial will pass away. When I was a child, I spoke like a child, I thought like a child, I reasoned like a child. When I became a man, I gave up childish ways. For now we see in a mirror dimly, but then face to face. Now I know in part; then I shall know fully, even as I have been fully known. So now faith, hope, and love abide, these three; but the greatest of these is love (1 Corinthians 13:4–13).

When I was dating I tried to view a relationship from the outside so I could see my friend for who he was. I prayed to God to show me what he was really like. God answered that prayer.

Read Proverbs 31:17–22. What word is found in each verse that depicts this woman as one who loved herself? Discuss the merit there.

_____

_____

> **Abstinence**—the fact or practice of restraining oneself from indulging in something.

SHE DOES HIM GOOD, NOT HARM

What husband would not want a wife who is actively seeking his good, not just sometimes but always.

"She does him good, and not harm, all the days of her life (Proverbs 31:12). That means no sex before marriage! I taught my children that sex is a God-given beautiful thing, but it is a fire. The fire in the fireplace gives warmth to the whole house, but the fire raging out of control destroys the house. The only container strong enough for sexual "fire" is marriage. Paul said, "For it is better to marry than to burn with passion" (1 Corinthians 7:9).

Start your courtship in purity, and then live God's way by doing your husband no harm.

Place "G" for good, and "H" for harm in front of the following deeds, and list others as well.

_____ Spending leisure time with male friends, when you have a husband.

_____ Educating yourself regarding household economics.

_____ Respecting the husband's opinions when not in agreement.

_____ Flirting with other men when you have a husband.

_____ Staying too busy to make the home top priority.

_____ Working to out-think, out-do, outsmart, and out-talk the husband.

Interestingly enough, nowhere in Proverbs 31 is there a description of the worthy woman's outward beauty. On the contrary, look what it does say about outward actions and appearance: "Charm is deceitful, and beauty is vain, but a woman who fears the Lord is to be praised" (Proverbs 31:30).

But she does work out. "She dresses herself with strength and makes her arms strong" (Proverbs 31:17). In fact, she does not just do workout routines, she "flat out" works. Verses 13–22, 27, and 31 all speak of her hard work and creativity.

Intelligence, hard work, and kindness are all far more lasting than beauty. But ladies, it is so unfair to attract a mate, and then once you have him, you go to seed. I have exercised every day since my first pregnancy. I realized that with a baby I would be too busy to go to a gym, so I used the time I took a shower as my exercise time. At age 24, I would step in place 24 times or do 24 leg lifts or other easy movements. Each year, I have increased my steps and other activity. These days I am really getting a good workout. I rarely park near the store where I shop. I use a pedometer, and I walk five miles a day. Lately, my favorite exercise is walking on the treadmill while listening to an audio book. I have developed this habit because a good book lures me to exercise!

Search Proverbs 31:10–31 for physical and spiritual activity. List in the columns below; then add your comments with additional scripture that supports balance in our "exercise."

Physical	Spiritual

TONGUE BRIDLING

"She opens her mouth with wisdom, and the teaching of kindness is on her tongue" (Proverbs 31:26). How many times has the teaching of kindness been on our tongues lately? If everything we said to each other were kind, there would be no divorce courts. Sometimes the ones we love the most get the roughest treatment, especially with our words.

Other Bible versions use "law of kindness" rather than "teaching of kindness." Research the meaning of that phrase. How can we learn to be kind? Find a verse in the New Testament that commands kindness.

_____

_____

QUESTIONS ABOUT YOUR GUY

Courtship is most certainly about being the best person you can be. The only person you can change is yourself. When you are dating, consider that if you are trying to impress him, he most certainly is trying to impress you. Beware of the "too charming" man. Remember this fact: if there is something now that you do not like, that quality will probably never get better. It is likely to get worse. Look at him and ask these questions:

❀ *Does he have long-term friendships?* If he has no friends but you because he has fallen out even with his family, how will he function in a forever thing like marriage? I used to attract people who needed my help. But in the end I realized that I needed someone secure and happy in himself.

❀ *Is he secure and happy in himself?* No man can depend on happiness from a source outside himself, so if he is depending on you to make him happy, back away!

❀ *Will he help me get to heaven?* If he is regular in church attendance, Bible study, and prayer when you are with him but shows little concern for spiritual things when you are away, he is not spiritually authentic. When you become forever obligated to him, he is likely to go back to his football and fishing when you are doing something he doesn't enjoy.

❀ *Am I willing to have children with this man?* As obvious as it might seem, most women don't always see the characteristics of their future husband as a part of their children. My husband was 17 years older than his youngest brother, and he was great with children and babies. He also had a very special relationship with his mother. He talked with her, and he communicated great with me.

Love is a powerful force, and it hit me like a ton of bricks. If you determine important criteria before marriage because you acknowledge God and know that He is the most powerful force of all, your marriage will be most blessed.

> *T*HE ONLY PERSON YOU CAN CHANGE IS YOURSELF.

I pray for my family. Do you? And I pray for the generations to come. As a Christian, I have come to believe that parents should pray a lot for the courtship and marriage of their children.

SHIPWRECK When David looked down from the highest rooftop in Jerusalem to a neighbor's rooftop, he lusted for a naked beauty. He satisfied his desires and brought mayhem to his family. His was not so much a courtship with Bathsheba but an "Oh no, what can I do so I won't get caught." But Nathan the prophet brought a message from God that shattered his hope: "The sword shall never depart from your house" (2 Samuel 12:10).

What an announcement, but it did come true. Amnon, David's oldest son, lusted for his half-sister and forced her to submit to him. Absalom, another son, murdered Amnon in revenge.

Later Absalom conspired against his father and made a desperate attempt to seize control of the government. David's army, operating under Joab, the field commander, went after him. David was deeply concerned for Absalom's welfare: "Deal gently for my sake with the young man Absalom" (18:5). But David's men were distressed. So it happened that one of Joab's men came upon Absalom hanging from the thick branches of an oak tree—his mule had run under that tree and Absalom's head got caught in the branches. A soldier ran and told Joab. Joab went straight to the oak tree, took three javelins, and thrust them through Absalom's heart.

FORGIVEN... BUT HIS SIN STILL HAD CONSEQUENCES.

When a runner came to David, the king asked anxiously, "Is it well with the young man Absalom?" (2 Samuel 18:29). The runner refused to answer, claiming there was a commotion and he was unable to determine what happened.

Then another runner, a Cushite, arrived. "Is it well with the young man Absalom?" David asked again.

The Cushite was honest and ready to answer: "May the enemies of my lord the king and all who rise up against you for evil be like that young man" (v. 32).

David was heartbroken. "O my son Absalom, my son, my son Absalom! Would God I had died instead of you. O Absalom, my son, my son!"

I am not saying that David was completely to blame for each of these travesties, but our sins have consequences even after we are forgiven. My friend's mother gave this advice on her daughter's wedding day: "Watch what you say in anger. It may be forgiven but not forgotten."

Guard yourself from all moral tragedy. When a moral shipwreck occurs, its ruins are long lasting, often eternal.

> "Now therefore the sword shall never depart from your house, because you have despised me and have taken the wife of Uriah the Hittite to be your wife." Thus says the Lord, "Behold, I will raise up evil against you out of your own house. And I will take your wives before your eyes and give them to your neighbor, and he shall lie with your wives in the sight of this sun" (2 Samuel 12:10–11).

David was forgiven but his sin still had consequences. His relationship with Absalom, from the time he took revenge on Amnon for forcing his sister Tamar until Joab ran three javelins through his heart, was a shipwreck. Some sons do not walk in the ways of their father, but most do. Let's be wise in our courtship.

SHIP'S LOG

1. Are you are dating someone now? Imagine him as an old man with coarse white ear hair and as deaf as a post. Now visualize yourself as his constant companion.

2. List your personal qualities. Are you in love with yourself? Remember, if you do not love yourself, you cannot love your neighbor or anyone else.

3. Do something very special for your special someone. Share with the class the results of your putting him first.

CHAPTER NINE

MOTHER-SHIP
MARY, JESUS' MOTHER

There is nothing more beautiful than a mother as she looks at her newborn baby. She engages with him with eyes full of love as she kisses his fingers and toes. There is nothing sweeter than the sound of a baby's laughter. A baby is the closest thing to heaven on earth. Is it not fitting that God sent His Son to be born of a virgin and that He would have a most special mother?

Let us examine scriptures to see the kind of mother Mary was.

- *Mary was faithful.* She believed the angel Gabriel, saying, "Behold I am the servant of the Lord. Let it be to me according to your word" (Luke 1:38). This was after the earth-shattering news that she, a virgin, was going to produce a baby by the Holy Spirit! Contrast this with Zechariah, the priest, who doubted the angelic proclamation that Elizabeth, his barren wife who was "advanced in years" would also produce a child (Luke 1:18). Doubt is the antithesis of faith.

- *Mary was pure.* She was a virgin. This is a precious thing to give your husband. No gift can compare. Marriages based on purity and God's will are blessed marriages. Even though Mary was pure, she was falsely accused. Has that ever happened to you?

Do what Joseph did. He did not "know" his wife until after she gave birth to a son named Jesus (Matthew 1:19–25).

✺ *Mary glorified God.* The longer I live the more I see that God's being glorified is essential to the happy Christian life. My daily prayer is that God be glorified. That way you see His power at work (Luke 1:46–55). Mary's song began with, "My soul magnifies the Lord, and my spirit rejoices in God my Savior" (vv. 46–47).

> And we all, with unveiled face, beholding the glory of the Lord, are being transformed into the same image from one degree of glory to another. For this comes from the Lord who is the Spirit (2 Corinthians 3:18).

According to 2 Corinthians 3:18 above, how can we expect to be transformed into God's image?

_____

✺ *Mary was joyful* (Luke 1:47). "Rejoice always" (1 Thessalonians 5:16). It is great to be around joyful people. Their joy can radiate and lift you up. Mary was that joyful. She was a "give God the glory" kind of girl.

Mary's spirit rejoiced in God. And "rejoice always" has the ring of a command—not a suggestion. Yet it is difficult to imagine that Mary was always happy. What is the difference between happiness and joy?

_____

_____

✹ *Mary was humble and yet accepting of her blessings* (Luke 1:48). She was not a queen in a palace, but a young girl from a despised place called Nazareth. "Nathanael said to him, 'Can anything good come out of Nazareth?'" (John 1:46). When Jesus preached in the synagogue in Nazareth, the townspeople rose up to throw Him off a cliff! Jesus had been raised there. His would-be executioners knew His mother, father, and siblings. (Luke 4:28–29). Can you imagine what kind of thugs lived in that town? As it turned out, they were religious thugs.

✹ *Mary acknowledged God in reverence.* "For he who is mighty has done great things for me, and holy is his name" (Luke 1:49).

Study Solomon's prayer at the dedication of the temple (1 Kings 8:22–61). Then study Hezekiah's prayer as he begged God for an extension of his life (Isaiah 38:1–3). Notice the reverence with which these men approached and implored God. How can we increase our reverence?

_____

_____

Mercy—an outward manifestation of pity; compassion shown toward someone whom it is within one's power to punish or harm. With the exception of Galatians 6:16, when mercy and peace are used together in scripture, mercy precedes peace, because peace in the heart results from divine mercy manifested toward man.

✹ *Mary put her trust in God to be merciful.* Mary acknowledged God's mercy in her song of praise: "And his mercy is for those who fear him from generation to generation" (Luke 1:50). Doesn't it seem that Mary would have been inclined to show mercy because she had received it? We know that God expects us to show mercy: "For judgment is without mercy to one who has shown no mercy. Mercy triumphs over judgment" (James 2:13).

God is the giver of every perfect gift, and one of those is mercy. I surely want Him to show mercy to me, a miserable sinner. And He is doing that for His children. He is covering our sin with the blood of His dear Son when we walk in His way. Read 1 John 1:7. What a wonderful God! And think of this: not only for my sins will He do that, but for generations to come. Pray for your children to be faithful, and also for their children and theirs. That way we are "praying it forward."

How does Luke 1:38 reflect Mary's trust in God? Select a song about God's mercy and sing it every day for a week.

_____

_____

Mary was neither a gossip nor a braggart. "But Mary treasured up all these things, pondering them in her heart" (Luke 2:19). She was obedient to the law of God (Luke 2:39). Are you a "ponderer"? A braggart? It seems that the human reaction to seeing your child in a discussion with scholars would be to say, "That's my boy!" But instead, Mary questioned Him.

Could it be that Mary was familiar with Proverbs 26:20? Fill in the blanks:

"For lack of wood the _____ goes out, and where there is no _____, quarreling ceases."

> **Wisdom**—insight into the true nature of things; the ability to view modes of action with a view to their results; the ability to think and act using knowledge, experience, understanding, common sense, and insight.

Mary may have homeschooled her Son. This homeschooling thought is near to my heart!

> And the child grew and became strong, filled with wisdom. And the favor of God was upon him (Luke 2:40).

How do we get filled with wisdom? Listen as Solomon speaks to his son: "Hear, my son, your father's instruction, and forsake not your mother's teaching" (Proverbs 1:8). We know that as Jesus was maturing, He increased in wisdom and stature and in favor with God and man. He was also trained in scripture, and in his young years it is safe to say that Mary helped Him, for at age twelve He amazed the Jewish teachers who heard Him in the temple. Wisdom comes from studying and constantly practicing the word of God. Jesus did that.

> For the word of God is living and active, sharper than any two-edged sword, piercing to the division of soul and of spirit, of joints and of marrow, and discerning the thoughts and intentions of the heart (Hebrews 4:12).

> For everyone who lives on milk is unskilled in the word of righteousness, since he is a child. But solid food is for the mature, for those who have their powers of discernment trained by constant practice to distinguish good from evil (Hebrews 5:13–14).

Jesus was absolutely wonderful in His ability to use God's word. When He was confronted by Satan with the "stones to bread" temptation in the wilderness, He quoted Deuteronomy 8:3, "It is written, 'Man shall not live by bread alone, but by every word that comes from the mouth of God'" (Matthew 4:4). Two more times in that context, Jesus shows that He had memorized scripture and could recall needed texts at will. Knowing scripture "by heart" is a dying art. We should teach our children to memorize God's word. Young brains absorb verses quickly and efficiently. Keep on training your children as Jesus' mother must have done.

Sometimes we hear, "Make the Bible come alive!" According to Hebrews 4:12 it *is* alive. What are some steps that we can take to truly own that thought?

_____

_____

Mary suffered as a mother. She was at the cross. She witnessed her baby boy's death, but she also saw Him after the resurrection. She was truly a humble, precious woman. Her humility was one of her greatest traits. She embodies each of the beatitudes. She was humble, faithful, and sweet, longing only for God's glory. Her needs were not important. She would never have wanted to be deified or worshiped. She was simply a godly woman who raised a godly Son. I want to be more like her.

In light of James 1:2–4, how can we view Mary's suffering? Discuss verse 4 with regard to Mary's evolving maturity.

_____

_____

Rebecca Harp Hooper, Emma Skype Hooper,
Gabriel Harp, Mary Harp, James Harp

SHIPWRECK We see Mary as a humble, sweet, loving girl. She did not gossip or seek her own way but wanted to humbly glorify God. She was at the cross and with the disciples after Jesus died. Mary was loyal and faithful to the end.

In stark contrast is Herodias, the wife of Herod, who was once married to Herod's brother, Philip I. Incidentally, Philip was Herodious' uncle; her father, Aristobulus, and Philip were brothers. Yikes! Imagine being at their family reunion!

John the Baptist preached against their union. Herodias, far from being humble or glorifying God, thought only to glorify herself. And she brought her daughter into the conspiracy. On one occasion when Herod was celebrating his birthday and was probably feeling his wine, Salome evidently performed a provocative dance in order to get what her mother wanted. And Herodias wanted John the Baptizer's head on a platter. What kind of woman would even think about putting her daughter in that position! Herodias would. She was wicked and conniving. She was determined to entice her husband, Salome's stepfather or great uncle—take your pick—to do her lurid bidding.

Herod had listened to John's preaching, and he feared the people who knew John was a prophet. He did not want to kill John, but because of his oath and the people who witnessed his promise, he carried out the execution.

Again, what kind of mother would ask her daughter to bring her a man's severed head on a platter? I'd like to have heard that therapy session. Wouldn't you?

Today, Herodias would be the queen of immorality. Her incestuous, adulterous, immoral ways are a stark contrast to the purity of our Savior's mother, Mary.

SHIP'S LOG

1. How might we become better at treasuring things in our hearts instead of gossiping?

2. How many Bible verses do you know by heart? Try putting desired Bible verses to song.

_____

_____

_____

_____

_____

CHAPTER TEN

MEMBERSHIP
SALVATION'S CALL

Our ship has made a remarkable journey. Rather like an explorer of yesteryear we have marked our passage by stopping along the way to gather provisions for the voyage ahead. An explorer needs also to chart his course so others can follow. Considering the fact that Captain Cook's only navigational instruments were a sextant and compass, he made very accurate maps of New Zealand. The Bible is our map book on our epic adventure to heaven. I would be remiss if I ended this journey without an in-depth look at how we get there.

> He has made everything beautiful in its time. Also, he has put eternity into man's heart, yet so that he cannot find out what God has done from the beginning to the end (Ecclesiastes 3:11).

We are spiritual beings.

Compile evidence that leads you to believe that mankind has an eternal nature. Use secular history, as well as your Bible.

~ BODY AND SOUL ~

> Then the Lord God formed the man of dust from the ground and breathed into his nostrils the breath of life, and the man became a living creature (Genesis 2:7).

God gave mankind something special that was not given to animals: "God breathedness." Solomon described it as eternity in man's heart. That explains why we are frustrated with the human condition. We are spirit beings locked in physical bodies—we are limited! The mind can transport us anywhere. In a nanosecond I can be in New Zealand ten thousand miles away or twenty years in the past or imagining a future event. There is no way the body can catch up with the mind. We also have that need to know, to stretch beyond what we have and are already. Yet two things conspire against us.

1. *Our physical limits.* "Yet you do not know what tomorrow will bring. What is your life? For you are a mist that appears for a little time and then vanishes" (James 4:14).

2. *Our separation from God.* "Behold, the Lord's hand is not shortened that it cannot save, or his ear dull, that it cannot hear; but your iniquities have made a separation between you and your God, and your sins have hidden his face from you so that he does not hear" (Isaiah 59:1–2).

So man has a separation problem called sin: "For all have sinned and fall short of the glory of God" (Romans 3:23).

What is the solution? Thankfully, our wonderful Father has provided the answer. By His grace He sent His Son.

For God so loved the world, that he gave his only son, that whoever believes in him should not perish but have eternal life. For God did not send his Son into the world to condemn the world, but in order that the world might be saved through him (John 3:16–17).

In times past, it was difficult to find even a child who could not quote John 3:16 from memory. The King James Version was most often quoted, "that whosoever believeth in him should not perish, but have everlasting life." God has provided love for the world, His only Son, and eternal life. Now, what is my part?

～ WHOSOEVER MEANETH ME ～

God made provisions so that I "should not perish." He gave me a part to play right there in John 3:16: believe in Him.

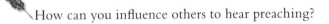 *I must believe that Jesus is God's Son.* A once-familiar hymn extolled, "Whosoever surely meaneth me!" You and I are the "whosoever" who believes in Him.

However James wrote, "You believe that God is one; you do well. Even the demons believe—and shudder!" (James 2:19). We know that demons are not saved. They believe and shudder because they know God's power but do not obey Him. Ours must be an obedient belief.

> How then will they call on him in whom they have not believed? And how are they to believe in him of whom they have never heard? And how are they to hear without someone preaching? . . . so faith comes from hearing, and hearing through the word of Christ (Romans 10:14–17).

How can you influence others to hear preaching?

_____

Why do those who have never heard of the true God believe in a higher being?

_____

How can those who grew up with a Bible in their hands claim to have faith, when they believe and practice a doctrine not found in the Bible?

_____

⌒ CHURCH DOORS UNLOCKED ⌒

Acts 2 is a record of Peter's preaching the first sermon after Jesus had risen. Jesus had already given Peter the keys to open men's minds to the kingdom of heaven (Matthew 16:15–19). Every person heard that sermon in his own dialect, as Peter opened the kingdom doors with the keys that Jesus promised when He assured the building of His church.

> Simon Peter replied, "You are the Christ, the Son of the living God." And Jesus answered him, "Blessed are you, Simon Bar-Jonah! For flesh and blood has not revealed this to you, but my Father who is in heaven. And I tell you, you are Peter, and on this rock I will build My church, and the gates of hell shall not prevail against it. And I will give you the keys of the kingdom of heaven, and whatever you bind on earth shall be bound in heaven, and whatever you loose on earth shall be loosed in heaven" (Matthew 16:15–19).

Peter made an accusation against his audience and presented a solution for sin:

> "Let all the house of Israel therefore know for certain that God has made him both Lord and Christ, this Jesus whom you cruci-fied." Now when they heard this they were cut to the heart, and said to Peter and the rest of the apostles, "Brothers, what shall we do?" And Peter said to them, "Repent and be baptized every one of you in the name of Jesus Christ for the forgiveness of your sins, and you will receive the gift of the Holy Spirit" (Acts 2:36–38).

The audience heard, and three thousand souls obeyed and were added to the church immediately. What a mighty congregation gathered inside those opened "doors" that day! (Acts 2:41–47).

⚓ *I must repent of my sins.* The word *repent* is not so often used in our day-to-day conversation.

> **Repent**—literally, to perceive afterward in contrast to perceiving before; to feel or express sincere regret or remorse about one's wrongdoing or sin. In the New Testament it signifies a change of mind for the better.

So when these Jews gathered on Sunday in Jerusalem for the Pentecost feast, they heard Peter preach. He convinced them that they had killed the Messiah, the Promised One, the Son of God. As sins go, that one was enormous! Yet our darling, gracious, heavenly Father stood ready to forgive even that huge sin. The perpetrators had to repent, turn around in their thinking, in order to serve God (Acts 3:19).

✼ *I must confess with my mouth that Jesus Christ is God's Son.* "So everyone who acknowledges me before men, I will also acknowledge before my Father who is in heaven" (Matthew 10:32). Note also:

> Because if you confess with your mouth that Jesus is Lord and believe in your heart that God raised him from the dead, you will be saved. For with the heart one believes and is justified, and with the mouth one confesses and is saved (Romans 10:9–10).

We believe, repent, and confess because we want eternal life. We want God to hear us. We should not allow our sins to separate us from Him. Jesus is the key.

✼ *Be baptized into Christ for forgiveness of sin.* We have already seen in Acts 2:38 that Peter told every person in his audience to repent and be baptized in the name of Jesus Christ for the forgiveness of their sins. Forgiveness is what we need. Baptism is wonderful. It moves us. *Moves us?* you may ask. Yes, baptism moves us from one state of being to another. It moves us from the darkness of sin into the blessed light of Jesus Christ. "For as many of you as were baptized into Christ have put on Christ" (Galatians 3:27). If you put on a jacket, you are inside that jacket. If you put on Christ, you are inside Him, clothed and covered by Him. To be in Christ is definitely where we want to be.

WHY BE IN CHRIST?

For the Lord himself will descend from heaven with a cry of command, with the voice of an archangel, and with the sound of the trumpet of God. And the dead in Christ will rise first. Then we who are alive, who are left, will be caught up together with them in the clouds to meet the Lord in the air, and so we will always be with the Lord (1 Thessalonians 4:16–17).

So Paul again says, "Therefore I endure everything for the sake of the elect, that they also may obtain the salvation that is in Christ Jesus with eternal glory" (2 Timothy 2:10).

But how do we get into Christ? "Into" denotes movement. When we walk into a house, we move from the outside to the comfort and safety of the inside.

Paul wrote,

Do you not know that all of us who have been baptized into Christ Jesus were baptized into his death? We were buried therefore with him by baptism into death, in order that, just as Christ was raised from the dead by the glory of the Father, we too might walk in newness of life. For if we have been united with him in a death like his, we shall certainly be united with him in a resurrection like his (Romans 6:3–5).

"Baptism, which corresponds to this [Noah's salvation by water], now _____ you, not as a removal of dirt from the body but as an appeal to God for a good conscience, through the resurrection of Jesus Christ" (1 Peter 3:21).

"Then Philip opened his mouth, and beginning with this scripture he told him the good news about Jesus. And as they were going along the road they came to some _____, and the eunuch said, 'See, here is water! What prevents me from being _____?' And he commanded the chariot to stop, and they both went down into the _____, Philip and the eunuch, and he baptized him. And when they came up out of the water, the Spirit of the Lord carried Philip away, and the eunuch saw him no more, and went on his way rejoicing" (Acts 8:35–39).

From Acts 8:35–38, mark these statements true or false:

_____ Baptism was an immersion.

_____ Baptism was cupping the hand and dribbling water over the head.

Baptism is a burial in water. We must be buried just as Jesus was. We go down into the water and, mimicking His resurrection, we rise up out of the water, cleansed from sin. We know that water has no power to cleanse us spiritually. The power of water alone is that of taking a bath.

In Christ, we are forgiven because our sins have been washed away. But I am a person, and I continually mess up. Does God say anything about that? Oh, yes He does.

But if we walk in the light, as he is the light, we have fellowship with one another, and the blood of Jesus his son cleanses us from all sin (1 John 1:7).

In this passage, "cleanses" means that His blood is continually cleansing. So if we are trying, that is, walking in the light, Christ's sacrifice is covering our sins.

MEMBERSHIP

Let's look at our membership in Christ's church. "So those who received his word were baptized and there were added that day about three thousand souls" (Acts 2:41). Also, "And the Lord added to their number day by day those who were being saved" (Acts 2:47).

True or False

_____ Membership in the church depended on the vote of other members.

_____ The early converts went before a committee to obtain approval for membership.

_____ God adds us to His church when we are saved.

_____ The early Christians were saved, then joined the church of their choice.

William and Brooke Harp McCurry, (Brooke holding baby James Harp), Mary Harp, Gabriel Harp, Richard Harp, Jenny and Scott Harp

Our membership must be God-approved. Let us follow the map of His word as accurately as possible so we will be together with God, the Father, and Jesus, our brother, in heaven. May God speed you on your journey across the sea. God bless you, and may you truly arrive ship-shape.

SHIPWRECK Among the saddest words in the New Testament are those of King Agrippa in Acts 26:28. Note those words in context:

> And as [Paul] was saying these things in his defense, Festus said with a loud voice, "Paul, you are out of your mind; your great learning is driving you out of your mind." But Paul said, "I am not out of my mind, most excellent Festus, but I am speaking true and rational words. For the king knows about these things, and to him I speak boldly. For I am persuaded that none of these things has escaped his notice, for this has not been done in a corner. King Agrippa, do you believe the prophets? I know that you believe." And Agrippa said to Paul, "In a short time would you persuade me to be a Christian?" And Paul said, "Whether short or long, I would to God that not only you but also all who hear me this day might become such as I am—except for these chains" (Acts 26:24–29).

The King James Version puts Agrippa's response this way: "Almost thou persuadest me to be a Christian."

That reminds me of the scribe in Mark 12:28. He walked up while Jesus was so fluently dealing with the Sadducees' question, "In the resurrection, when they rise again, whose wife will she be?" The scribe's question was, "Which is the first commandment of all?" Jesus answered by giving him both the first commandment and the second commandment. He commended Jesus, and Jesus responded, "You are not far from the kingdom of God." It's that *not far,* that "so close but not quite there" attitude, that saddens us. We never see in scripture that King Agrippa's *almost* became *altogether.*

Salvation means that death is the next step to a great adventure. *Almost* means calamity. Being saved is the most important thing in life.

SHIP'S LOG

1. Write a paragraph describing your salvation.

2. Ask yourself if your "salvation experience" is in line with God's word.

3. Express some ways you are walking in the light. Share with the class.

_____

_____

_____

_____

_____

_____

_____

_____

_____

_____

_____

_____

_____

CHAPTER ELEVEN

CITIZENSHIP
BEATITUDES ARE FOR ME

Sometimes our ship takes us on the most memorable journey. Ours docked at a delightful port in Scotland recently where our son and his beautiful wife presented us with our first grandson! During this time, I spoke to the ladies' class of the East Kilbride Church of Christ. I love those ladies, and I loved studying this citizenship lesson with them. This lesson was greatly influenced by a sermon by Dan Winkler. I had especially struggled with these concepts, but they became very simple as I sat at Dan's feet. I want very much to be a citizen of heaven, so I am very happy to understand and practice the deep lessons of Christ.

> Blessed are the poor in spirit, for theirs is the kingdom of heaven.
>
> Blessed are those who mourn, for they shall be comforted.
>
> Blessed are the meek, for they shall inherit the earth.
>
> Blessed are those who hunger and thirst for righteousness, for they shall be satisfied.
>
> Blessed are the merciful, for they shall receive mercy.
>
> Blessed are the pure in heart, for they shall see God.

Blessed are the peacemakers, for they shall be called sons of God.

Blessed are those who are persecuted for righteousness' sake, for theirs is the kingdom of heaven.

Blessed are you when others revile you and persecute you and utter all kinds of evil against you falsely on my account. Rejoice and be glad, for your reward is great in heaven, for so they persecuted the prophets who were before you (Matthew 5:3–12).

Let us now focus on the characteristic of each challenge. The first three beatitudes are the prerequisites to becoming a Christian, the next four are about Christian conduct, and the final ones are the worth of being a Christian and what you are willing to do for Christ.

~~~~~ AM I HUMBLE? ~~~~~

"Blessed are the poor in spirit, for theirs is the kingdom of heaven" (Matthew 5:3). Jesus did not say, *blessed are the poor,* because that would exclude the middle class and the wealthy. Neither did He say, *blessed are those with a spirit.* That would be all inclusive, as we all have that inner man, that eternity in our hearts (Ecclesiastes 3:11).

That spirit He alludes to is the spirit that says, *I absolutely need my God. I could do nothing without His Son Jesus. I am nobody without God's Holy Spirit, and I am bereft without the family of God, His church.* Sisters, this is the spirit of humility. It is only the humble that will accept God's word as the official map to traverse life's sea. This attitude of heart is the very essence every woman needs to become a Christian. Luke 18:9–14 illustrates this humility.

"God, be _____ to me, a _____"
(Luke 18:13).

Humility Serves

Do you know a humble woman? She will seek an opportunity to serve others. She will love her neighbor as herself. James tells us what pure and undefiled religion is. He does not mention baptizing thousands, being a missionary traveling the world, or being a writer of Bible commentaries. Rather, he says,

> Religion that is pure and undefiled before God, the Father, is this: to visit orphans and widows in their affliction, and to keep oneself unstained from the world (James 1:27).

Visit—to look upon or after, to inspect. That doesn't sound like our kind of "visit," does it? Actually, the Greek root of the word is close kin to the root of *episkopos*, 'overseer,' used to describe the work of congregational elders. What is their job? To inspect the flock and lead it to a better relationship with God.

> Do not be conformed to this world, but be transformed by the renewal of your mind, that by testing you may discern what is the will of God, what is good and acceptable and perfect. For by the grace given to me I say to everyone among you not to think of himself more highly than he ought to think, but to think with sober judgment, each according to the measure of faith that God has assigned (Romans 12:2–3).

I wish you could meet Bea, a precious lady who worships with us. She embodies the humble, poor-in-spirit person. She has had some tough knocks—buried her husband and all her children—but she loves her God and her church family and goes about serving others in a gentle, sweet way. She truly embodies the beatitudes.

In addition to Romans 12:3, find at least one more scripture that tells us how to think. Why is a woman's thinking so important?

How does Philippians 2:4 teach that the selfish woman has a service/humility problem? Copy the text here.

~~~ DO I SORROW FOR SOULS? ~~~

"Blessed are those who mourn, for they shall be comforted" (Matthew 5:4). I struggled with this verse until I learned that Jesus had a particular kind of mourning in mind. It is sorrow caused by sin. A sinner must mourn and have godly sorrow because of personal sin in order to become a Christian.

> Now when they heard this they were cut to the heart, and said to Peter and the rest of the apostles, "Brothers, what shall we do?" (Acts 2:37).

Cut to the heart? Literally "stabbed down." They were stabbed in the heart when they learned that the man they killed was the Messiah, God's only begotten Son, and they were desperate to make amends. Their mourning produced good results. It was not mere lip service, saying "sorry," but a deep remorse that required action. "What can we do? We have killed the Lord Jesus. Help us!" I'm paraphrasing, but it means the same. Peter's response was, "Repent and be baptized . . . " (Acts 2:38).

What a glorious God we serve. He is willing to forgive us completely when we obey Him. He is also willing to give Himself to all who repent. And with His blood, He will wash away our sins in baptism. If that is not love, I do not know what is!

Find the example of the young man who spoke with Jesus, yet "went away sorrowful." How was his sorrow different from the mourning of those in Acts 2? Contrast the end result of each.

_____

_____

_____

~~~~ AM I MEEK? ~~~~

"Blessed are the meek, for they shall inherit the earth" (Matthew 5:5). I am ashamed to say that I used to think that "meek" meant "weak." Actually, the opposite is true. A wild stallion that has been tamed is still strong and fast, but he is submissive. He uses his inborn abilities in the service of his master. Meekness is strength under control.

Medicinally, "meek" is medicine that goes down smoothly. It also describes a characteristic of someone who is gentle with others. The meek know they have a master. They know that others should be treated with kindness. Those who are strong, kind, and submissive to God will benefit from His blessings.

The first three beatitudes—humility, sorrow for sin, and submission to God—describe what it takes to become a Christian. The next four involve Christian living.

Why do you think Moses was described as meek?

_____

What Bible woman showed this strength under control?
(1 Samuel 25).

_____

Find other specific biblical examples that show meekness and
discuss them.

_____

_____

AM I
～～ RIGHTEOUSNESS-STARVED? ～～

"Blessed are those who hunger and thirst for righteousness, for they
shall be satisfied" (Matthew 5:6). Have you ever been hungry, truly
hungry? I have. True hunger is when the desire for food is not a want
but a need. I prayed and God provided. We are to seek after God's
word. It is like vital life-giving nourishing food without which you
would die. His promise is that we will be satisfied, and that satisfac-
tion comes only from God's word. Earthly life is a vapor, so dissat-
isfying, but God's righteousness promises eternal life. There can be
nothing more satisfying than eternal, loving joy. Read James 1:5, 17.

Jesus used the common appetite to teach a vital principle.
Challenge a friend to a day of fasting. With every thought of
food, consider that craving in contrast with your craving for
spiritual food.

∼∼∼∼∼ AM I MERCIFUL? ∼∼∼∼∼

"Blessed are the merciful for they shall receive mercy" (Matthew 5:7). The original meaning of mercy carries with it the idea of getting into another person's skin. A familiar quote is, "Grace is getting what we do not deserve; mercy is not getting what we deserve." We benefit from God's grace and His mercy. He knows us inside our skin and outside, and He is merciful. When we are judgmental and harsh, we're not showing mercy.

"For judgment is without mercy to one who has shown no mercy. Mercy triumphs over judgment" (James 2:13).

Do you want God's judgment or His mercy? If you truly empathize with another person, that is, see things from her point of view, you will act more kindly and lovingly toward her.

I spent my early years trying to get the approval of others. Sometimes when people do not want peace with you, no matter how loving you are, all you can do is what you can do.

Paul wrote, "If possible, so far as it depends on you, live peaceably with all" (Romans 12:18). Some people do not want peace with you. What can you do when that happens? Change yourself. If you are trying to please them, stop! You cannot please the unpleasable. You need only to please God. The rest will take care of itself. Stop letting their "think so's" control you. The results will be better.

SOME PEOPLE DO NOT WANT PEACE.

Try to be merciful. For whatever reason, some folks are unable to receive love. Change your attitude. Only God, Jesus, and the Holy Spirit are perfect. Everyone else will disappoint you because we are all imperfect, frail human beings. Your happiness must be in God's hands, not another person's. God will carry you through.

~~~~~ AM I PURE IN HEART? ~~~~~

"Blessed are the pure in heart, for they shall see God" (Matthew 5:8). The heart has much to do with our thinking. We must retrain our thinking. I battle depression, and Philippians 4:5–9 is my rescue passage. Read those verses. During times of struggle, before my feet hit the floor in the morning, I play Philippians 4:8 in my mind. It is especially meaningful to me; during the day I rehearse it often:

> Whatever is true, whatever is honorable, whatever is just, whatever is pure, whatever is lovely, whatever is commendable, if there is any excellence, if there is anything worthy of praise, think about these things.

Friend, whatever is true is whatever is real. Many of our depressing thoughts and fears are imagined, so learn to focus on what is real. God made me. God loves me. God sent His Son for me. Heaven is real, and heaven is my goal. This life is a vapor. God is real! "Blessed are the pure in heart, for they shall see God." When you focus on God's word, you keep God in your daily life. You see God in good times and bad.

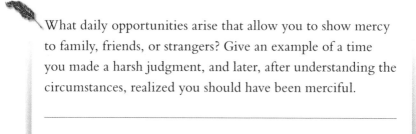

What daily opportunities arise that allow you to show mercy to family, friends, or strangers? Give an example of a time you made a harsh judgment, and later, after understanding the circumstances, realized you should have been merciful.

_____

_____

~~~~~ DO I PURSUE PEACE? ~~~~~

"Blessed are the peacemakers for they shall be called the sons of God" (Matthew 5:9). And close behind is another dimension of persecution:

> Blessed are you when others revile you and persecute you and utter all kinds of evil against you falsely on my account. Rejoice and be glad, for your reward is great in heaven, for so they persecuted the prophets who were before you (Matthew 5:11–12).

The Son of God was labeled "Prince of Peace" centuries before His birth. We women often live in a chaotic sea and long for peace. And yet we are not just to wish and long for peace, we are to diligently pursue it, according to 1 Peter 3:11. This very verse that says, "Turn away from evil and do good," also states, "Seek peace and pursue it." Also Romans 14:19 says, "Pursue what makes for peace and for mutual upbuilding."

How often do we open our mouths and out pops something derogatory, demeaning, and totally thoughtless? Do we forget that the same Bible that commands repentance and baptism also commands us to put discipline to work to make peace? O be careful, mouth, hands, feet, and ears! Let's walk in the way of peace and be children of God.

Ponder the following words of our Savior:

> Peace I leave with you; my peace I give to you. Not as the world gives do I give to you. Let not your hearts be troubled, neither let them be afraid (John 14:27).

If Jesus left His peace with us, how are we applying it to our lives? Many of our hearts are troubled and afraid—just the opposite of Jesus' admonition!

How do you reconcile Matthew 10:34–36 with the "peacemaker" beatitude?

_____

_____

What are some ways that Christian women pursue peace?

_____

_____

Research the background of John 14:27, and write your findings here.

_____

_____

Just as Jesus left us peace to prevent fearful and troubled hearts, Paul also soothes us with the promise of peace when we follow these instructions:

> Do not be anxious about anything, but in everything by prayer and supplication with thanksgiving let your requests be made known to God. And the peace of God, which surpasses all understanding, will guard your hearts and minds in Christ Jesus (Philippians 4:6–7).

AM I PERSECUTED?

"Blessed are those who are persecuted for righteousness' sake, for theirs is the kingdom of heaven." Blessings and happiness come when you are persecuted (Matthew 5:10). Heaven is beyond our expectations. Heaven is worth persecution. And God, His Son, and His word are worth the effort. God does not ask us to do anything He was not willing to endure.

Read 2 Timothy 3:12–13. To whom is persecution promised? What did Paul have to say about his persecutions? (v. 11).

_____

_____

We often sing "This world is not my home" to inspire us to endure trials and trust God to rescue us. How does Philippians 3:20–21 prove that a Christian is an alien on earth?

_____

_____

Dad, Captain Edward L. Hubbard

When our ships encounter storms and rough winds, we often label our sufferings "persecutions." But are we being persecuted for right-doing? Are we suffering a consequence of some action? Or is our suffering the result of sin? Regardless, we do suffer on stormy seas. In these struggles, remember the words of Hebrews 12:4: "In your struggle against sin you have not yet resisted to the point of shedding your blood." Remember our ultimate example in the person of Jesus who suffered persecution for righteousness' sake. Look to Him as you patiently guide your ship toward the port.

> Let us run with endurance the race that is set before us, looking to Jesus, the founder and perfecter of our faith, who for the joy that was set before him endured the cross, despising the shame, and is seated at the right hand of the throne of God (Hebrews 12:1–2).

Hallelujah and amen!

 **SHIPWRECK** To be poor in spirit is not for everyone. Jesus met a very successful young man—as the world defines success—who was everything but poor in spirit. In fact, he was wealthy in spirit, and that wealth was conceived and maintained by his abundance of material wealth. He was a Jew who thought his life was absolute perfection. You know that young man, but let's review his encounter with Jesus.

> And behold, a man came up to him, saying, "Teacher, what good deed must I do to have eternal life?" And he said to him, "Why do you ask me about what is good? There is only one who is good. If you would enter life, keep the commandments." He said to him, "Which ones?" And Jesus said, "You shall not murder, You shall not commit adultery, You shall not steal, You shall not bear false witness, Honor your father and mother, and, You shall love your neighbor as yourself." The young man said to him, "All

these I have kept. What do I still lack?" Jesus said to him, "If you would be perfect, go, sell what you possess and give to the poor, and you will have treasure in heaven; and come, follow me." When the young man heard this he went away sorrowful, for he had great possessions. And Jesus said to his disciples, "Truly, I say to you, only with difficulty will a rich person enter the kingdom of heaven" (Matthew 19:16–23).

How different he was from Saul of Tarsus after he acknowledged his Savior on the road to Damascus and put Him on in baptism three days later. Saul was ready to give his all for the Lord, and he did. He gave up his Jewish name and adopted a Roman name—Paul. He gave up his countrymen, and many times he forfeited his security and well-being to deal with problems among his fellow Christians, but he never complained. "Christ Jesus came into the world to save sinners," Paul said, "of whom I am the foremost." Paul was poor in spirit. What a blessing!

The rich young ruler thought he had it all, but he lacked the humility and faith to inherit eternal salvation. He lacked the will to give it all away and follow Jesus. That's what it takes. We must be willing to serve the One who has the words of life.

> WE OFTEN LABEL OUR SUFFERINGS "PERSECUTIONS." ARE THEY?

Whatever you do, don't turn away from Jesus. Abandoning Him will bring great sorrow. Your citizenship in heaven is worth whatever it takes to maintain a relationship with Him. To have that citizenship, we must be poor in spirit.

SHIP'S LOG

1. Plan to show mercy to someone—perhaps a child in your class or a grumpy coworker. Try to empathize and go the extra mile for that person.

2. How can we be peacemakers? Share ideas with the class.

_____

_____

_____

_____

_____

_____

_____

_____

_____

_____

_____

_____

_____

_____

_____

_____

_____

_____

CHAPTER TWELVE

ONE-UPMANSHIP
HEBREWS—GOOD, BETTER, BEST

A sleek beautiful ship docks at the port. It is the newest and best. It is our "one-upmanship." The old song with the lyrics "I can do anything better than you" is the idea introduced in one-upmanship. Usually *one-upmanship* has a negative connotation, because we know it is not nice to brag. But we women often have the tendency to compete with one another. Who keeps the best house? Who prepares the best meals? Whose children are the best behaved?

The book of Hebrews teaches us that without Jesus we are nothing. For Him, you might say, "No brag, just fact." This section of scripture sets out to examine how Jesus is most excellent, above all others. People of the day in which it was written needed its encouragement to keep the faith, and so do we.

> Long ago, at many times and in many ways, God spoke to our fathers by the prophets, but in these last days he has spoken to us by his Son, whom he appointed the heir of all things, through whom also he created the world. He is the radiance of the glory of God and the exact imprint of his nature, and he upholds the universe by the word of his power. After making purification for sins, he sat down at the right hand of the Majesty on high, having become as much superior to angels as the name he has inherited is more excellent than theirs (Hebrews 1:1–4).

Jesus Christ is better than the prophets, because God appointed Him as heir. He is also the means by which the world was created. No prophet could make that claim. Read John 1 and Colossians 1. He is better than angels.

Now note what the Hebrews writer says about Him:

> He makes his angels winds, and his ministers a flame of fire. But of the Son he says, "Your throne, O God is forever and ever, the scepter of uprightness is the scepter of your kingdom" (Hebrews 1:7–8).

So Jesus is better than angels because they are ministering spirits, whereas He is God.

Study Hebrews 2:5–19 from ESV and other translations. When was Jesus lower than the angels? How was that status for Him temporary? How was it "fitting for Him"? (v. 10).

_____

_____

_____

SUFFERING, CONQUERING, SAVING

Jesus Christ is the founder of our salvation. He brought that salvation about through suffering that He might empathize with us as a better high priest (Hebrews 2:17–18).

He suffered for our sake and became the pearl of great price. Think about the pearl. A sharp grain of sand enters the oyster's shell and irritates the tender flesh. The oyster begins quickly to grow a shiny skin around the intruder. Then he grows another and another until a beautiful smooth gem glistens there. (Read Matthew 13:45–46.) The pearl is perfected by suffering. Similarly, suffering brought about in Jesus the beauty of salvation (Hebrews 5:8–9). Christ's salvation is better than any other. It is perfect, complete, and worth everything! Heaven's gate of pearl is another metaphor for that glorious salvation wrought for us by our Savior's pain.

"And being made perfect, he became the source of eternal _____ to all _____ _____ _____" (Hebrews 5:9).

How does the religious world often teach a doctrine that leaves out the last three words of that verse?

_____

_____

CHAINS OF DEATH

Christ is also the better avenger.

> Since therefore the children share in flesh and blood, he himself likewise partook of the same things, that through death he might destroy the one who has the power of death, that is the devil (Hebrews 2:14).

So Jesus has defeated the devil for us. He has broken the chains of death. And because He has experienced humanity, He is empathetic to our plight.

Now read Hebrews 2:15. Write it here, with your comments.

_____

_____

~~~ MOSES, AARON, PRIESTS ~~~

Christ is better than Moses, Aaron, and the priests of Levi (Hebrews 3:3). Years ago I read *Pilgrim's Progress* to my kids. Something stands out in that story that explains the law of Moses in contrast to Christianity. A man named Christian walked past a room. Inside, a man was busy sweeping. Great clouds of dust flew around the sweeper. That room represented the Mosaic law that was designed to expose sin, and it did that well. But it was never intended to be the solution for sin.

TIME OF NEED? RECEIVE MERCY. FIND GRACE.

In the next room, a man was on his knees, with a soapy bucket. He was permanently removing dirt from the floor. This was meant to show the superiority of Christ's sacrifice over Moses'. Christ is man's solution for sin. He is truly greater than Moses.

Jesus is a better High Priest than Aaron was because He is able to sympathize with our weaknesses. Jesus was tempted like we are, yet He endured without sinning—He never sinned! (Hebrews 4:14–16). Now He offers mercy. We deserve judgment, but our wonderful High Priest in the person of Christ paid our debt. "Let us then with confidence draw near to the throne of grace, that we may receive mercy and find grace to help in time of need" (Hebrews 4:16).

Jesus was of the tribe of Judah. According to the law of Moses, priests came from the tribe of Levi. Jesus' priesthood was different and better. "You are a priest forever after the order of Melchizedek" (Psalm 110:4). Who was Melchizedek? He was the king of Salem in Abraham's day. Abraham had defeated king Chedorlaomer and the kings with him, rescuing his kinsman, Lot. Melchizedek, the king of Salem and the priest of God most high, blessed Abraham (Genesis 14:18–20). Abraham made a free-will offering of a tenth of everything to this priest. (Read Hebrews 7:1–10.) This priest's qualifications were not connected with a particular lineage, as were the priests under the Mosaic system. Additionally, the twelve tribes were in place after Abraham, so Levi didn't exist in Abraham's time. Like Melchizedek, Jesus is both priest and king. Jesus is the better priest because "He entered once for all into the holy places, not by means of the blood of goats and calves but by means of his own blood, thus securing an eternal redemption" (Hebrews 9:12).

"For we have not an _____ _____ which cannot be touched with the feeling of our infirmities; but was in _____ points tempted like as we are, yet without _____" (Hebrews 4:15 KJV).

What are some of the "infirmities" or weaknesses that we experience? How do they tempt us to sin? Why should this verse provide strength in troubled times?

_____

_____

Jesus is our high priest, touched by our infirmities. But He is also our _____ (1 John 2:1). What does His being an advocate mean to you?

_____

~~~~~~~ ONCE FOR ALL ~~~~~~~

Jesus' covenant is better because it is eternal. His covenant is a once-for-all kind. It was secured with His own pure blood at His death. He did not enter a tent made with hands, but He went into heaven. His sacrifice secured the salvation of those who had gone before—Abel,

Enoch, Noah, Abraham, and all others. His gift enables everyone to be cleansed from sin and to be saved eternally (Hebrews 9:28).

Let us consider how amazing our God is. He sent His Son, who is also God, to be clothed with humanity for us! Jesus knows what it is to be hungry and cold. He knows how to submit to others when all should submit to Him. He knows how to obey and to serve others.

We cannot grasp God's omniscience, omnipotence, or omnipresence. Those qualities are unlike us. We can only imagine what it is like to be everywhere at once as we plod along in our finite bodies, bound to time and space, as irresistibly as a magnet is bound to steel. Neither can we fully grasp the all-powerful God. A category-five tornado can sweep away everything in its path. It can push pine needles through concrete. It is often described as the "finger of God"! His power, might, and majesty, make us feel ant-like, dwarfed, and trembling. Recall Moses' going up on the mountain and the people's fear of the God who made Moses' face glow so that he had to wear a veil in their presence (Exodus 34:33–35). God is powerful.

> THE MONSTROUS BACKPACK OF EARTHLY CARES SOMETIMES WEIGHS US DOWN.

But this powerful God chose to be born as a tiny, fragile baby, with ten toes and ten fingers for a mother to kiss, in order that we could have a relationship with Him. What a supreme example of His love! How could an omniscient, omnipotent, and omnipresent Being condescend to being spat upon? (Matthew 27:30). How did He let spittle and tears trail down His cheeks when He had the power to destroy in a nanosecond the angry, evil mob that was brutally going to kill Him? What unfathomable love!

But for the joy of heaven, Jesus went to the cross so that I—me, tiny ant me!—could be in heaven with Him!

> **Once for all**—That phrase translates a single Greek word, *ephapax*. While the King James Version usually translates it as "once," other versions give the more definite translation. English Standard Version has it this way in Romans 6:10: "For the death he died he died to sin, *once for all*, but the life he lives he lives to God."

Using a concordance or search engine, find at least three biblical references that use the term "once for all." How do these verses confound those who teach a new revelation by new prophets? Also, contrast the "once for all" sacrifice Jesus made with the animal sacrifices made under Moses.

_____

_____

_____

ENDURANCE COACH
AND ENCOURAGER

Jesus also provides the example of better endurance (Hebrews 12:1–3). Jesus has run the race and won it, therefore we can also run our race and win. Not only did Jesus carve the way through treacherous terrain and made the path straight, He is also our running coach and chief encourager. We can imagine Jesus' whispering, *Do not give up! Do not give up! Do not give up! The prize is in sight.*

What a prize it is, too! It is heaven; freedom from the monstrous backpack of earthly cares and concerns that we all carry, the pack that sometimes weighs us down. Jesus' prize is better than the worldly prize of sin and death. The curse of death has been broken. Keep on keeping on the path of our Lord to the end, because heaven is worth it all. That is what the Hebrews writer tells us. One-up-manship is awesome when we are in Christ! The next time you are tempted to strive to be better in a haughty or superior way, stop! Then pray that Jesus Christ will be glorified by what you do.

A farmer once showed me his farm. He stretched out his hands and moved them as to sweep them across his land and said, "Look what I have done." Deep inside I sighed because I knew something he did not know. Without God there would be no grass, no trees, and no life! In life we might accomplish great things, acquire great wealth, and enjoy extraordinary accolades, but Christ makes all pale in comparison. One-upmanship is about perspective. When Jesus enters the discussion, all other successes find their way to the back of the line.

How does Hebrews 12:1–11 link endurance with discipline? Read these verses every day for a week. At the end of that week, answer this question: What effect did this reading have on my attitude?

_____

_____

_____

Consider him who endured from sinners such hostility against himself, so that you may not grow weary or fainthearted.
—Hebrews 12:3

SHIPWRECK The book of Hebrews talks about the superiority of Jesus over Moses. The reason? Moses was faithful in God's house as a servant. Jesus was faithful over God's house as a Son, and Jesus was the builder of that house (Hebrews 3:1–6). Jesus is truly the Son of God.

But what of Herod (Acts 12)? He was a great political figure and had been raised to great heights by God Himself. The terms *poor in spirit, humility, subjection,* and the like were foreign concepts to Herod.

> Now Herod was angry with the people of Tyre and Sidon, and they came to him with one accord, and having persuaded Blastus, the king's chamberlain, they asked for peace, because their country depended on the king's country for food. On an appointed day Herod put on his royal robes, took his seat upon the throne, and delivered an oration to them. And the people were shouting, "The voice of a God, and not of a man!" Immediately an angel of the Lord struck him down, because he did not give God the glory, and he was eaten by worms and breathed his last. But the word of God increased and multiplied (Acts 12:20–24).

The inspired historian gives us the gist of Herod's plight in few words. Eaten of worms? Yuk! Herod's arrogance led to his humiliating downfall and the termination of his life.

As for me, I choose poverty in spirit that results in spiritual blessings a thousand times over arrogance in life that results in worms and curses from the Almighty. And I will stake my claim on God's promise:

For it was fitting that he, for whom and by whom all things exist, in bringing many sons to glory, should make the founder of their salvation perfect through suffering.
—Hebrews 2:10

SHIP'S LOG

1. How do you glorify Jesus in what you do? Your job? Your marriage? Your home? Through your children?

2. List some of life's pursuits that are generally considered excellent. Then discuss what happens when these pursuits are examined under the light of Christ's superiority.

_____

_____

_____

_____

_____

_____

_____

_____

_____

_____

_____

_____

_____

_____

_____

_____

_____

CHAPTER THIRTEEN

FELLOWSHIP
STIRRING UP GOOD WORKS

I used to think of fellowship in a loose sense, that of sharing and bonding over interests, often with food at our gatherings. Fellowship to me was also associated with my favorite books of all time, *The Lord of the Rings*. My favorite part of the trilogy is *The Fellowship of the Ring,* where friends go forth together on a quest. The world is eventually made safe from evil when the ring is destroyed. And they truly bonded because of their one purpose.

As a Christian I grew to appreciate the bond of fellowship with my Christian sisters. I especially love bonding during ladies' retreats. I have collected several large envelopes over the years from those events where we wrote encouraging notes to everyone at the retreat. I have pulled these out and reread them many times. Each time I am reminded of a special bond between Christian sisters.

> **Fellowship**—joint participation, association, community. One aspect of fellowship in the New Testament was "breaking bread at a common table."

~~~ ALL THINGS IN COMMON ~~~

Let's examine fellowship in Acts 2, because that is where we may realize a deep meaning.

> And with many other words he bore witness and continued to exhort them, saying, "Save yourselves from this crooked generation." So those who received his word were baptized, and there were added that day about three thousand souls. And they devoted themselves to the apostles' teaching and the fellowship, to the breaking of bread and the prayers. And awe came upon every soul, and many wonders and signs were being done through the apostles. And all who believed were together and had all things in common. And they were selling their possessions and belongings and distributing the proceeds to all, as any had need. And day by day, attending the temple together and breaking bread in their homes, they received their food with glad and generous hearts, praising God and having favor with all the people. And the Lord added to their number day by day those who were being saved (Act 2:40–47).

~~~ SAVE YOURSELVES! ~~~

First, Peter exhorted the people on Pentecost to "save yourselves from this crooked generation." That is going to be the key to our need for fellowship, a bond of strength we get from sisters and brothers.

They needed to bond together in fellowship for physical protection, because persecution was imminent. The Jews hated this new sect, and the Romans hated the purity of Christians, so Nero blamed them for the burning of Rome.

"And all who believed were together and had all things in common." Their love for Christ and belief and subsequent action of being baptized into Him made these first-century Jews unique. They were immediately family.

Remember, they came from all over the world for the Pentecost feast in Jerusalem. Now they were thrown together and saved by a single belief in Christ. Many stayed in Jerusalem because that is where their new brothers were. That meant they were away from their homes, and they had needs.

Salvation is provided by Jesus, yet Peter told those Jews at Pentecost to save themselves (Acts 2:40). In what sense could they do that?

_____

_____

CARING AND SHARING

What an out pouring of love! Barnabas and others shared land and wealth. They gave of their plenty to supply the lack of their brethren.

> There was not a needy person among them, for as many as were owners of lands or houses sold them and brought the proceeds of what was sold and laid it at the apostles' feet, and it was distributed to each as any had need. Thus Joseph, who was also called by the apostles Barnabas (which means son of encouragement), a Levite, a native of Cyprus, sold a field that belonged to him and brought the money and laid it at the apostles' feet (Acts 4:34–37).

They physically came together. This is an important ingredient to fellowship for us. We get too busy and tear around madly, doing our own thing. If all the contact we have with Christians is on Sunday morning, we will miss this wonderful thing called fellowship.

I remember inviting a couple who visited our services to our house for lunch. I was shocked when the woman told me they had not been to someone's home for a meal in fifteen years! We need to get back to meeting in our homes. That's where we can extend love and hospitality, and bond together.

At our congregation we have a wonderful group called Supper Club. We sign up with two other families to meet in our homes. Older couples mix with young families that otherwise would not meet socially; the results are precious. Usually in our Bible classes and often in social gatherings we meet in our age groups, but we need to stretch that concept and, like the Christians in the first century, come together.

And like them, our purpose should be to encourage and build up each other. If we bond in fellowship, we are more likely to remain faithful.

Discuss the pros and cons of meeting only in age groups. How does the practice of peer-grouping limit fellowship?

_____

What alternatives might promote more fellowship?

_____

_____

Is fellowship the only issue, or could doctrine be involved?

_____

~~~~ SPECIFIC FELLOWSHIP ~~~~

I love *Lads to Leaders / Leaderettes* because I see fellowship extending with the purpose of helping our kids. There is something exciting about seeing thousands of young people participating in speeches, puppets, and Bible bowl. But what is thrilling is that kids who come through that program are more likely to stay faithful. They see that they have a real part to play now, not just in the future. *Lads to Leaders / Leaderettes* trains children.

> Train up a child in the way he should go; even when he is old he will not depart from it (Proverbs 22:6).

Lads to Leaders / Leaderettes also highlights fellowship—our oneness. We are all important; no one should be elevated above another in the church. Seek out someone who you can make feel special and loved. If you are lonely, look outward and strengthen the bond.

How may a focus on children unite grownups?

_____

_____

What are other ideas for training our youth?

_____

_____

List at least two actions that you are able to perform in teaching youth.

_____

_____

A MIND TO WORK IN MISSIONS

One of the best ways to bond in fellowship is to go into the mission field together. I see churches most active in fellowship doing this. It thrills my heart to see families taking vacations, not to Disney World but to Nicaragua and other poor countries. There is a deep fellowship as we serve the less fortunate. The youth bond too—kids who have so many material blessings work with children who have nothing but seem so happy. It's a spiritual lesson in contentment that is learned through experience.

Research the value of work in bonding Christians together. Cite scripture references.

_____

_____

Discuss the focus of working in other countries. Write a scripture that describes the primary focus. How do some groups stray from the primary focus? What steps might prevent a mission group from losing its focus?

_____

_____

_____

NO WAVERING WHILE STIRRING

If we get fellowship right, we will strengthen each other in the gospel. We will not see each other only in a church foyer but we will be a force for God. Fellowship is important. We need each other. The world needs to see that no matter what hardship befalls us, there is joy and a family in Christ.

> Let us hold fast the confession of our hope without wavering, for he who promised is faithful. And let us consider how to stir up one another to love and good works, not neglecting to meet together, as is the habit of some, but encouraging one another, and all the more as you see the Day drawing near (Hebrews 10:23–25).

Make your own stirring list. How will you promote love and good works? A strong word, *neglect,* is used to stress the importance of meeting together. How does assembling stir up love and good works?

_____

_____

_____

SHIPWRECK

> But a man named Ananias, with his wife Sapphira, sold a piece of property, and with his wife's knowledge he kept back for himself some of the proceeds and brought only a part of it and laid it at the apostles' feet. But Peter said, "Ananias, why has Satan filled your heart to lie to the Holy Spirit and to keep back for yourself part of the proceeds of the land? While it remained unsold, did it not remain your own? And after it was sold, was it not at your disposal? Why is it that you have contrived this deed in your heart? You have not lied to man but to God." When Ananias heard these words, he fell down and breathed his last. And great fear came upon all who heard of it. The young men rose and wrapped him up and carried him out and buried him (Acts 5:1–6).

Barnabas gave willingly to help brothers and sisters who struggled. He showed that he had given his heart to God first. Ananias and Sapphira wanted merely to appear spiritual and giving, so they lied.

Our fellowship must be real and we must not be concerned with how we look to others. Appearances are secondary. Genuine love and bonding are keys to true fellowship, not neglecting to meet together, as is the habit of some, but encouraging one another (Hebrews 10:25).

In scripture, fellowship is linked to staying faithful. If we neglect coming together we will corrode the bond of strength. The lone stick is easily broken, but try snapping a bundle of sticks. The larger the bundle, the greater the resistance. In unity we have strength. If we strive for fellowship as they did in Acts 2, we will stay united in Christ.

SHIP'S LOG

1. Take a moment to write something positive about everyone in class. At the end of class everyone will have a large envelope of encouraging notes to take home. You, like me, will never throw them away.

2. You might realize that you cannot write very much because you do not know everyone. Purpose to get to know someone better. Take her to lunch. Strengthen the bond of fellowship.

_____

_____

_____

_____

_____

_____

_____

_____

_____